BREAKING the perfect 10

daytime television star of the bold and the beautiful, one life to live and sunset beach

tracy Lindsey meLchior

with susan waLes

BREAKING the perfect 10

BROADMAN
& HOLMAN
PUBLISHERS

NASHVILLE, TENNESSEE

10-digit ISBN: 0-8054-3262-0
13-digit ISBN: 978-0-8054-3262-6

Published by Broadman & Holman Publishers
Nashville, Tennessee

Dewy Classification: B
Subject Heading: MELCHIOR, TRACY \ ACTRESSES—
BIOGRAPHY \ HOLLYWOOD (CA)—RELIGIOUS

Although this is a true story, some names have been changed
to protect those actually involved.

Unless otherwise noted, Scripture quotations are taken from
the Holman Standard Christian Bible (HCSB), copyright © 1999,
2000, 2002, 2003 by Holman Bible Publishers. Other versions
include *The Message*, the New Testament in Contemporary
English, © 1993 by Eugene H. Peterson, published by NavPress,
Colorado Springs, Colo. and the New Living Translation (NLT),
copyright © 1996. Used by permission of Tyndale House
Publishers, Inc., Wheaton, IL 60189 USA. All rights reserved.

1 2 3 4 5 6 7 8   09 08 07 06 05

To the men in my life, my husband Rob and my son Kyle, evidence of God's grace and love.

TRACY LINDSEY MELCHIOR

To my family for their love and support: my husband Ken, my daughter Meg, my granddaughter Hailey Elizabeth, my parents, the Hueys, and my heavenly Father for his gifts and blessings.

SUSAN WALES

Acknowledgments

With deepest gratitude to David Shepherd and Len Goss of Broadman & Holman Publishers for the opportunity to share my story and the message of Jesus Christ our Savior with others. Thanks to both of you and my agent Ted Baehr for somehow knowing I had something to say, and not perpetuating the stereotype that "pretty blondes are meant to be seen and not heard." Thanks to Susan Wales for helping me organize my thoughts well enough to create a book and for always believing in the book even when I had my doubts. Also thanks to Kim Overcash for being a great project editor and counselor during the whole production/publishing process.

Thanks to Jeffery David and Pastor Dave Stockline for that one hour on Sunday, you changed my life. To Chris Chauncey and Scott Reichent for introducing me to your friend Jesus, and Heather Taylor as well as everyone else who encouraged me to keep going and to have no fear. Also for my sisters and parents for allowing their lives to be exposed so God could be glorified.

And to Rob, for being the kind of husband that allows me to be the kind of wife God wants me to be.

Table of Contents

Introduction

Therefore if any one is in Christ, there is a new creation;
old things have passed away, and look, new things have come.

—2 CORINTHIANS 5:17

O nce upon a time I was an actress who lived in a superficial
world in Tinsel Town. Today I am an actress who lives in a
supernatural world in God's kingdom. I didn't find peace and happiness in Hollywood, but strange as it may seem, I found God
there. Now instead of acting for an audience of fans, the producers, the director, and the press, I act for an audience of one. Today
the only review that matters to me is God's review of the life I'm
living.

As a result, I have not only lived happily ever after, but I also
know that I will live for an eternity because I know Jesus Christ
as my Lord and Savior. Having lived in both worlds I can tell
you that I now cling to Christ's great promise: *I assure you: Any-*
one who hears My word and believes Him who sent Me has eternal
life and will not come under judgment but has passed from death to life
(John 5:24).

Since the evolution of Hollywood, society has transformed its celebrities into our gods. We worship them, watch them, envy them, support them, cheer them, and read about them. Americans are obsessed with Hollywood and its stars. Many actors are attracted to the profession for the adoration and approval from audiences and fans. Sadly, they rely on these mere human beings for their self-worth. No wonder so many actors crash and burn on this slippery slope. For many actors, happiness is based on the latest review or the feedback from the last audition.

For years I lived a life that would please man instead of God.

It's cool to be an actor, especially a successful actor. Successful actors make gobs of money, wear beautiful clothes, live in mansions, drive fancy cars, and do and say whatever they please. Did I mention that people worship celebrities? Who wouldn't want to be a star?

Yet not everyone can succeed as an actor in Hollywood. Climbing the ladder of success in Hollywood is a brutal journey where few ever reach their destination to the stage, the small screen, and especially the silver screen. Hopefuls get trampled in the process of trying to get there and fall off the ladder. Others are bruised, battered, and wounded by the time they reach their goal. Then there are those few who float magically to the top.

The number of people who succeed is a small percentage. I've heard that only 5 percent of the actors in The Screen Actor's Guild make more than $5,000 per year! Can you imagine trying to survive in this profession? Few actors who make it to the top in Hollywood stay there long. I think Mary Astor said it best in her book, *A Life on Film*:

Five stages in the life of an actor . . .

1. Who is Mary Astor?
2. Get me Mary Astor.
3. Get me a Mary Astor type.

4. Get me a young Mary Astor.

5. Who's Mary Astor?

I've had minor success as an actor, and I am grateful that God has blessed me with an opportunity to work in the industry since I'm so passionate about acting. I never take what little success I've had for granted, because fame, like beauty, quickly fades.

Actors often are referred to as the *beautiful people*. A requirement for most successful actresses is their looks. Often beauty is more important than talent when casting a job. Most people have to have talent to stay in the business for long, and even then there are exceptions, but physical beauty definitely opens the door for acting. I know it was my appearance and not my talent that landed me my first acting job.

Society worships beautiful women. When I was a young girl, it was a cool custom for guys to rate a girl's beauty by saying she's an eight or a five or whatever. Blake Edwards, the famed director who also produced and directed classic films such as *Breakfast at Tiffany's* and *The Pink Panther*, perpetuated this rating system with his movie *10*, starring the beautiful Bo Derrick.

A lot of guys played the game with their ultimate goal to find a *Perfect 10*, but few women qualified. So few existed that when a guy spotted a *Perfect 10* it was a big deal. You can only imagine my shock when I got to Hollywood and a man said to me, "Tracy, you've broken the *Perfect 10*."

Of course in my eyes I didn't qualify. But the rating and the attention flattered me. It was impossible for me even to consider myself attractive, much less even close to the *Perfect 10* because I felt so *imperfect*. I grew up so neglected that I not only believed I was ugly but also that I was invisible to others. I felt I had no worth. It wasn't until I begin to get attention from all the boys that I realized I was pretty.

Once I discovered that men found me attractive, my looks became more of a curse than a blessing. Beauty soon became a great source of power for me to attract the attention and affection I craved. Ultimately, my beauty has brought me far more pain than pleasure.

Most women would do almost anything to break the *Perfect 10*, but to me it was a symbol of pain, but not as painful as breaking God's *Perfect 10*. Until I was in my twenties, I had never even read the Ten Commandments. It's human nature for most people not to like rules, but God's commands offer us a guideline to live a more abundant life right here on the earth, and bring honor and glory to his name.

The Ten Commandments

Then God spoke all these words:

I am the LORD your God, who brought you out of the land of Egypt, out of the place of slavery.

Do not have other gods besides Me.

Do not make an idol for yourself, whether in the shape of anything in the heavens above or on the earth below or in the waters under the earth. You must not bow down to them or worship them; for I, the LORD your God, am a jealous God, punishing the children for the fathers' sin, to the third and fourth [generations] of those who hate Me, but showing faithful love to a thousand [generations] of those who love Me and keep My commands.

Do not misuse the name of the LORD your God, because the LORD will punish anyone who misuses His name.

Remember to dedicate the Sabbath day: You are to labor six days and do all your work, but the seventh day is a Sabbath to the LORD your God. You must not do any work—you, your son or daughter, your male or female slave, your livestock, or the foreigner who is within your gates. For the LORD made the heavens and the earth, the sea, and everything in them in six days; then He rested on the seventh day. Therefore the LORD blessed the Sabbath day and declared it holy.

Honor your father and your mother so that you may have a long life in the land that the LORD your God is giving you.

Do not murder.

Do not commit adultery.

Do not steal.

Do not give false testimony against your neighbor.

Do not covet your neighbor's house. Do not covet your neighbor's wife, his male or female slave, his ox or donkey, or anything that belongs to your neighbor.

(Exod. 20:1–17)

By the time I found God, I was horrified to discover that I had broken every single one of his *Perfect 10* commandments. Yes, even commandment number 6. It didn't matter to my heavenly Father how many of these laws I'd broken because God had sent his Son Jesus to pay the price for my sins. He loved me just the same with a love like no other, a perfect love I didn't have to work or manipulate to receive. Jesus met me right where I was.

When I found God, I fell on my knees to beg his forgiveness for my many sins and accepted his love, his mercy, and his grace. Jesus did it all for me. He can do it all for you too. He paid the price for my sins when he died on the cross of Calvary in order that I might have life eternally and that I might live my life here on the earth more abundantly.

After accepting Jesus Christ as my Lord and becoming obedient and adhering to his laws, my life has taken on a new meaning.

My life is worth living. Prior to my discovery, there were many times I felt it wasn't worth living and I didn't care if I lived or died.

How many of his laws have you personally broken? It doesn't really matter if you'll ask his forgiveness and invite him to be Lord of your life. You, too, can find such freedom, joy, and purpose in your life.

Fame is indeed fleeting, beauty fades, and physically we fail, but Jesus Christ offers life everlasting. Climbing the ladder of success in Hollywood is a brutal journey, and many never get there, but anyone who calls Jesus Savior and believes in him and confesses their sins can enter God's kingdom. It's a free gift because Jesus Christ has paid for your admission to eternity with his life. What love! What sacrifice!

As the pages of my story unfold, no doubt, my broken life may not be what you would expect. I felt a call to write this book to show that if someone like me, who has lived a life of sin and broken not one but all the Ten Commandments, can find Jesus and salvation, then you can too.

Chapter 1

Facades

❧❧❧

Where is Hollywood located?
Chiefly between the ears.
In the part of the American brain lately vacated by God.
—Erica Jong, *How to Save Your Own Life*

A great beginning for a soap star—I was born in Hollywood! Sounds glamorous, doesn't it? In truth, my birthplace wasn't the *real* Hollywood but a coastal city in Florida, nestled between Fort Lauderdale and Miami. Hollywood was the site selected by the 1920s visionary, Joseph Wesley Young, for his Dream City in Florida, only to have it blown away in a storm after he had built his city.

My parents had both grown up in Hollywood. My mother had matured into a beautiful redhead when she was crowned Miss Air Force at age thirteen. The next year she was crowned Orange Bowl Queen. It was no surprise that she had some serious suitors. At sixteen, she fell madly in love with my father, who was thirteen years her senior. Realizing it was impossible to keep the lovers apart, my grandparents eventually relented and allowed them to marry. My mother, only sixteen, had children right away: first my sister Robin, next Kristine, and two years later, I was born.

Though *our* Hollywood was on the east coast and we were a far cry from royalty, much less filthy rich, we were still dubbed a *celebrity* family by our friends and neighbors. My father was a cop with a beautiful wife and three lovely young daughters. Years later, in the 1980s, everyone referred to my two older sisters, Robin and Kristine, and me as "Charlie's Angels," the characters in the popular hit TV show by the same name. Joseph Fred Ort wasn't named Charlie, but he shared the same profession with the television character. He was one of Miami's finest, a cop, so "Charlie's Angels" was the perfect description for his girls.

People marveled at the likeness of the Ort's three beautiful daughters, miniature versions of the show's stars. Like Jaclyn Smith, my older sister Robin had a glorious mane of dark hair but with sparkling brown eyes; Kristine, our middle sister, was a dead ringer for Kate Jackson; and I was a blonde, blue-eyed mini-version of Farrah Fawcett.

Life was good for the Ort family. While our daddy was away chasing the bad guys, Mom stayed home with her angels and beloved dogs. In addition to being a mom, she also bred and showed Great Danes. Her profession instilled a love of animals in me from a tender age that would endure for a lifetime. It also afforded me the opportunity to learn about the miracle of life. My love of animals enabled me to survive in the rocky years to come.

Loving parents, pets, and maternal grandparents who lived nearby created the perfect formula for the large family I enjoyed during my first five years. Totally oblivious to the storm that was brewing all around me, I appeared to enjoy my life as a happy and healthy five-year-old, but like the real Hollywood, my life was all a facade. Behind closed doors, our home looked as though it had been hit by a hurricane. Our mother had little interest in being a homemaker. Christopher P. Johnson states in his book *The Power That Women Have*, "A women's home is an extension of herself. It is a reflection of heart and her soul."[1]

Our home was evidence of the chaos and decay in my mother's life. To make matters worse on the domestic scene, everything in our home revolved around the Great Danes my mother raised. Raising dogs was rewarding, but it had its downfall. The animals wreaked havoc on our home. It was more like living in a dog kennel than a house. Filled with dog crates, our home had little room for a child to move around. Although Great Danes are short-haired dogs, there is nothing else short or small about them; they have big slobbery drools and big bad smells. Their hair clung to our clothes and everything else in our home.

Growing up, we became so accustomed to living with the odors and the filth that we were oblivious to them. It's amazing how you get used to the smell of your house, and to you it doesn't even stink anymore.

Yet we knew our home was different, and we never dared to invite anyone inside. Our only visitors were an occasional rat or the roaches. Our parents both loved the dogs, and a clean house was never the priority that the animals were. Sadly, neither were their children more important than the animals.

Perhaps that's why an uncertain fear hovered over my early childhood years. I never understood what it was but only knew I felt insecure, apprehensive.

So much for happy endings. Would the facade crumble just as Joseph Young's city had? Hollywood's founder never saw his city restored to its original splendor after the storm, but what a legacy he left! Port Everglades grew from a shallow lake into one of the busiest seaports in Florida. God redeemed Young's dream even though he didn't live to see it, but the man will be long remembered for Hollywood, Florida. What would become of my future in Hollywood?

The winds of my personal storms first began to blow after my family took a summer vacation to the other Hollywood! Our father purchased a motor home for my mother to use when she went to dog shows, so we drove across the country in it for a family vacation. We drove up and down the California coast, stopping at sights along the way. Funny, it's Knots Berry Farm I remember, not Hollywood. A typical four-year-old, I wanted to experience all the fun life had to offer a child.

Only months before, our grandparents had moved from Hollywood to Colorado to live near their oldest son. We missed them terribly. Stopping by Colorado to visit our grandparents on our drive back to Florida, my sisters and I were especially delighted to see Nana and Pop-Pop and our cousin Eric. My grandparents adopted Eric, my Mom's oldest sister's son, when he was baby, and we had missed him too.

Playing outside, we could not ignore our mother, Nana, and Pop-Pop arguing inside. Ordinarily a kind and gentle soul, whenever Nana was around our mother, her whole demeanor totally changed. Apparently a long history of conflict and unresolved issues had existed between mother and daughter, but as children, we were shielded from most of their disagreements.

Our parents soon told us good-bye and told us to have a nice summer.

Nana reassured us as we watched our parents drive away, and we immediately began planning our adventures for the summer.

My sisters and I enjoyed a blissful summer at our grandparents' house that year. Yet when night fell and Nana and Pop-Pop tucked us in our beds and turned out all the lights in our room, I would pull the covers over my head and lie awake and think of my mommy and daddy. Like any child, I desperately longed for my parents and wanted to go home.

As summer came to a close, the back-to-school advertisements ran on TV, so the three of us began to ask our grandparents, "When are we going home?"

To our surprise they told us that we were going to enroll in school there. "What a great time you'll have at your new school," Nana said cheerfully.

I was deeply saddened by the news and longed for my mother and father. My grandparents had taken Eric from his mother, and now they obviously were going to take us from our mother and father too.

Nana and Pop-Pop had criticized their daughters so much that my mother and her sister truly believed that they were unfit mothers, so it was easy for my grandparents to convince my mother to leave us with them. She truly believed that she was doing what was best for her children. However, for a child there is no substitute for a mother and a father.

In a matter of weeks, the three of us were happily settled into the local school, making new friends. Both of our grandparents worked, so we would come home to an empty house in the afternoon; but the four of us, Robin, Kristine, Eric, and I had one another. It wasn't long until Nana came home and had dinner on the table.

In no time Colorado became our home, but our parents were missing from this picture of a family. I kept watching and waiting for them to show up one day, but as the days, then the weeks, and then months went by, they never did.

Standing in the garage one day, I sensed a presence. When I turned around, there was a beautiful woman standing there, smiling as though she knew me.

The stranger suddenly held out her arms to me and beckoned, "Aren't you going to give me a hug, Tracy?"

"Mom?" It couldn't be. I couldn't believe my eyes. Mom was thinner, prettier, and even sported a longer hairstyle. Had it been that long since I had seen her? Her shoulder-length hair had grown down past her hips. Once I recovered from the initial shock of seeing her again, I was overjoyed to see my mother. Mom loved to surprise us and with her unexpected reappearance, she succeeded. At last she had come back for her girls.

With our grandparents' disdain for our mother, I was afraid to voice my feelings of joy at seeing her again. Our grandparents had provided our care, so I didn't want to offend or appear ungrateful to them. Thus began my struggle to know where my loyalties should lie. When my mother wasn't around, my grandmother reacted with disgust if I ever dared say anything about missing her. Was something wrong with me because I had feelings for my mom and longed to be with her? I felt I had no choice but to suppress my feelings for my mother, and I truly believe this contributed to the total shutdown of my feelings from an early age. Torn between my loyalties to my mother and to my grandmother, I would do and say anything to please the one I was with, even if it meant disparaging the other. I also became adept at hiding my feelings for the other in order to please the one I was with. Were these the seedlings that later led to my adulterous personality?

A few days later when our father showed up at our door, demanding to see us, my grandparents refused to let him inside the house. In the past my grandparents had adored my father. No telling what my mother had told them. Subsequently, the adults spent most of their timing arguing. It was a frightening scene for three young girls.

My grandparents knew our mother wasn't perfect, but she was still their daughter. Although they sometimes expressed their doubts over my mother's truthfulness, they were afraid not to believe her allegations about my father and what had driven her from her marriage. My mother could be convincing when the situation called for it. In spite of the problems they had with her, my grandparents were in her corner on this one. I believe another reason they weren't welcoming to our father was they didn't want to lose us.

First, my mother showed up out of the blue. Next came my father's angst-filled arrival. I became more confused and anxious than ever. While life with my grandparents was nurturing, like any young child I continued to long for my parents and prepared to go home with both of them. Recent studies show that even abused children long to remain with their parents. Most young children will love and idolize their mother and father in spite of their shortcomings.

Although we were well cared for and loved by our grandparents, it was heartbreaking for us when our father left without us that day. Little children have big ears, and at times we overheard our grandparents badmouthing our mother. The only thing I ever heard them say about my dad was, "At least he sends the child support every month." I guess to them his money made up for whatever else he was supposed to have done, but to his children a few hundred dollars a month was no substitute for a father.

Our mother lingered a few more weeks with us, but one day, without a word, she disappeared again. It became apparent to me that my mother had chosen a life without us. Although Pop-Pop was a stern disciplinarian when my mother and siblings were growing up, he had mellowed in his old age, so my mother had obviously done something that upset him. She said later that my grandfather had thrown her out of the house, and she was forced to live at a cheap hotel and work as a waitress at a diner in order to survive.

Years later we asked our mother why she deserted us. Our mother explained that since the day we were born, her parents repeatedly told her that she was an unfit mother. Eventually she began to believe them. She was convinced that her children would be better off without her. My grandparents convinced her that it was best for her children if she went away and left her children with them. Not wanting to harm her children any more than her parents convinced her that she already had, our mother disappeared at frequent intervals in our lives.

We were loved and well cared for by our grandparents, so life at their home went on as usual with occasional visits from our mother and father. My father refused to give up custody and fought desperately to get his girls back. Eventually, the fighting wound down, and our father returned to Florida. He hadn't given up but was returning home to pack his things and move to Colorado to be near his girls.

Chapter 2

Without Shelter

Loss grew as you did, without your consent.

—ANNIE DILLARD, *An American Childhood*

The storms temporarily subsided when our father left the state and our mother stopped by on occasion. For the most part our grandparents were raising us girls. Our mother now had a new boyfriend who came along with her on her visits. Her boyfriend, John Lindsey, was a newscaster on the local CBS affiliate and a celebrity around Denver. Soon after we moved to Colorado that first summer, my mother met John at a country music gathering sponsored by a local radio station. Sadly, John's appearance on the scene extinguished any hope I had for my parents' reconciliation.

I will never forget the first time our mother pointed out John on the TV during his five o'clock newscast on CBS. I looked behind the TV and wondered, *How did John get in there?* From this day forward, a part of me knew that if I wanted to get my mother's attention, I'd have to figure out a way to get inside the TV box too.

As an adult I can clearly see that this moment is when the seed of my desire to become an actress was firmly planted inside my head and heart.

John said that he fell hopelessly and madly in love with my mother at first sight. He was a nice enough man but apparently had never wanted any children of his own. He always kept the three of us at arm's length, and my mother allowed it. Sometimes we were invited to spend time with John and my mother at his home where they lived together.

Mom and John would visit with us until Mom and Nana got into another one of their arguments, and then Mom would run and jump in the car, slam the door, and John would shrug his shoulders and follow her like a lovesick puppy. They'd drive off and not show up again for awhile.

We always looked forward to their visits . . . especially when they would take us to ride horses, which we loved. Having had our own horse in Florida, we developed a passion for the animals at a tender age. Although our mother was unable to ride due to a back injury she had sustained during a car accident, she had loved horses as a young girl.

I don't recall how much time had passed but eventually our father reappeared. To our surprise, he had someone with him— a new wife, our stepmother, Sharon. Her presence further cemented any chance for us to be a family again. Upon our father's return, his lawyers turned up the heat on the custody battle; nevertheless, it waged on and on. Even with the ongoing custody battle, my grandparents would occasionally allow our father and Sharon to visit us.

It wasn't long until Sharon began to complain about the cold weather in Colorado. Homesick for her native Florida, our stepmother grew tired of the frigid temperatures and begged our father to move back to the Sunshine State. Our father was becoming increasingly frustrated over my mother's and grandparents' manipulations and their refusal to allow him regular visits with his girls. At this time, fathers did not have the rights in the court system that they enjoy today. Eventually my father and his discontented wife packed up and moved back to Florida.

Although my father was far away, his battle for custody didn't cease; he continued to fight, but to no avail. Desperate to get his girls back, he tried another tactic. He wrote my mother a letter and told her that it wasn't in the girls' best interest for their growth and maturity for them to see her shacking up with John. My father offered to continue to pay my mother the child support if she would allow his daughters to come and live with him.

In a surprising turn of events, my mother agreed to allow Kristine and me to go live with our father. Because Robin was older, they agreed to allow her to make her own decision, and she chose to stay in Colorado. Dad and Sharon drove back to Colorado and picked us up in a motor home, and we drove across the country to Florida with them.

I still have fond memories of the exciting drive back to Florida. We stopped along the way to sightsee, singing the songs from the Barbara Streisand tape, *Guilty*, as we traveled down the highways of our great country. Having been deprived of living with our parents for so long, it was a big deal for my sister and me to be with our dad and stepmom.

Once we arrived in Florida, we were delighted to see that Dad and his wife had arranged two beautiful rooms for Kristine and me in their home. Our father had painstakingly handcrafted our bedroom furniture and even allowed us to pick out the color of the stain. He made me feel very special, something I hadn't felt in a long time.

Dad and his wife Sharon lovingly cared for us in every way. Sharon packed delicious and nutritious school lunches for us, and each night she would tenderly fold the blankets back on our beds for us and then tuck us in before she and Daddy would tell us that they loved us. It made such an impression on me that today I perform this same ritual when I put my son Kyle to bed at night.

I enjoyed living with my father and Sharon, but Kristine became desperately homesick. To make matters worse, we both had a difficult time adjusting to our new school, and this made Kristine even more miserable and eager to return to Colorado. Phone calls to our mother became a nightly ritual for my older sister as she pleaded with our mother to come and get us. She'd cry for hours on the phone and beg our mother to let us come home. Kristine said she desperately missed riding my mother's horses. While I loved the horseback riding, too, I was too young to be as passionate as Kristine was about the animals.

I'm sure it made my mom happy that we missed her. I was confused. I didn't know where I belonged, and I didn't want to have to choose. I was perfectly happy with Dad, but I missed my mother too. I didn't want to have to choose.

When she intimated to me that she would let me ride one of the horses in a horse show, which had always been my dream, I suddenly wanted to go home too. I was a child easily bribed by presents and promises. What child isn't?

In spite of the more conventional life I had in my father and Sharon's home, I now joined Kristine in her quest to return to Colorado. Besides, if Kristine had been successful in getting our mother to agree to her return, I would have never stayed in Florida without her. No matter what, Kristine and I stuck together.

My father and stepmother had gone to an exorbitant amount of trouble to make a home for us with them. Even as a child I felt really guilty about leaving them and being forced to pick a parent, but Kristine made the difficult choice for us. My father and Sharon admitted later that they were devastated when our mother finally made arrangements for us to return to live with Nana and Pop-Pop. Until I had my own child, I could not have imagined how deeply the loss of his children affected my father.

I know that my father fought desperately to be with his girls and that our return to Colorado hurt him deeply. Having become acquainted with my mother's manipulation as an adult, today I am sympathetic to his frustration over her games; but in my eyes, this does not change the fact that he, too, abandoned us when he left Colorado. Painful as it is to admit, my father must bear some responsibility for the neglect and abuse we received at the hands of our mother in the years to come since he was not there to monitor the situation. Had he made more of an effort to be there or visit on occasion, he would have known. Instead, when our father returned to Florida, the separation from him had tragic results in the lives of my sisters and me.

Even though we rejected our father when we begged to move back to Colorado, today as an adult, I believe he should have moved back to Colorado so he could visit us frequently or refuse to allow us to return to Colorado. He did not, and in the next fifteen years of my life I only saw him twice.

Back in Colorado, I never got any of the things that were promised to me by my mother. It was years later before I was finally allowed to show a horse. Upon our return we moved back in with Nana and Pop-Pop, and they provided a wonderful home for us. My sisters and I, along with my cousin Eric, led a happy life with Nana and Pop-Pop. Our grandparents took on the role of loving and nurturing parents with the offspring of their two rebellious daughters.

We loved having a "brother" around, and our cousin Eric had previously longed for siblings. Eric was delighted to have three sisters there. We were one big happy family for the next five years.

Life was good, but every night in bed I felt so guilty that a cloud of sadness veiled my heart. Even as a young child I realized that this darkness that hovered over me was my longing not only for my parents but also for my heavenly Father, but at the time I had no knowledge of him. I felt shame, believing that somehow I wasn't lovable. Had I been, my parents never would have divorced, nor would they have abandoned me. It was obvious to me that my mother wanted to get away from me, and my father didn't care enough to beg me to stay with him.

Throughout our childhood, we never had any religious training. Occasionally, Nana would mention God and say that she talked to him, but we figured he was just another friend of hers. I vaguely remember our grandparents taking us to church one Easter Sunday, but I can't recall any specifics about the event. Our Sundays were usually spent watching sports on TV, and during the football season our family congregated in the family room to cheer for the Denver Broncos. At halftime we would rush outside and play football.

The final year we spent at our grandparents' home was filled with sadness when Pop-Pop became ill. When he was hospitalized and diagnosed with diabetes, everything in our lives suddenly changed. Once home from the hospital, he was placed on a respirator. As the machine pumped air into his lungs, it pushed the joy out of our lives.

In spite of his illness, Pop-Pop insisted on giving us our allowance every Friday afternoon. Pop-Pop was a successful salesman and businessman and wanted to instill good business principles into the lives of his grandchildren. As soon as he dropped the change into our hands, we rushed out the door and down the street to the Barn Store, a convenience store in our neighborhood, and bought all the candy the money would buy, yet we still managed to save a nickel. Stewardship was just one of the many lessons he taught his grandchildren, and as an adult I am grateful for these valuable lessons. Throughout my life these lessons have served me well.

Pop-Pop became ill again, so they took him away to the hospital and he never came home again. With Pop-Pop's life hanging in the balance, no one remembered my birthday. I was devastated.

On June 22, I celebrated my tenth birthday alone during Pop-Pop's illness by singing "Happy Birthday" to myself in the bathroom mirror as tears streamed down my face. This would be the last time in my childhood that I allowed myself to cry, to feel. It would be years before tears came again.

By June 30, my birthday was completely forgotten when Nana told us Pop-Pop had died.

All of us deeply mourned our grandfather's passing. Pop-Pop was buried in a cemetery situated high on a Colorado mountain. A large cross at the top of that mountain burned brightly each night. It could be seen for miles around. At night I would look up at that cross and long for my grandfather who was buried on that mountain. God was clearly drawing my young eyes to the cross. How did I miss his mammoth example of showing me the light?

Pop-Pop's death was a tremendous shock to us, but the biggest shock was yet to come. Following Pop-Pop's funeral, our grief-stricken Nana came home, barely uttering a word to any of us. We stood in shocked silence as she began packing all of our things in large plastic garbage bags.

The realization suddenly hit my sisters and me. Not only had we lost our grandfather, but we were about to lose our home too. Where would we live? With our mother? This thought was thrilling to my heart, but I had learned long ago to squelch any hope where my mother was concerned. John had made clear that we couldn't live with them, and we already failed at living with our dad. Colorado was our home, but now we had nowhere to go.

Nana's behavior puzzled us, yet no one bothered to explain anything to us. No one ever answered our questions. I was later to learn that our uprooting had more to do with an argument between our grandmother and our mother than it had to do with Nana's rejection.

We stood speechless when Mom showed up and loaded the plastic garbage bags of our possessions into the trunk of her car. First Mom explained that Robin, who had become a rebellious teen, was going to move in with our aunt and uncle.

Initially, Kristine and I assumed that we would be moving in with our mom and John, but instead, on the day we moved out, she drove us to a house she had rented and told the two of us that this was our new home.

"I'll be back to check on you soon," she promised. Filling the cupboards with groceries, she kissed us good-bye and left.

We didn't question our mother's leaving us but resigned ourselves to the fact that this was our lot in life. We never questioned that our mother loved us; we knew she did, but we naturally assumed that she preferred John's company to ours. As a result, I felt that we just weren't lovable enough to keep my mother around for long. It took years for me to realize the profound psychological effects of my mother's abandonment and neglect upon my life.

Tragically, when Kristine and I were left home alone to fend for ourselves, we were only twelve and ten years old. Time passed, and Mom did not return. The isolation and loneliness became unbearable for me. Yet I trusted my mother completely. If she said she was coming back, then I believed her. I would have waited years for her to return to us.

Given our mother's history of popping in and out of our lives, truthfully her disappearance wasn't that unusual. It was just that this time we were left alone with no one to care for us. It was Nana's disappearance from our lives that surprised me the most. Why hadn't our grandmother come for us? For five years she had loved and cared for us. Where was she now? Adults need to be cognizant that if these types of things aren't explained to a child, then the child is forced to draw his own conclusions, and he usually assumes the worst. I assumed anybody I loved would leave.

Thankfully we had two dogs for security and as comforters. I truly believe this is why I have such an enormous respect and devotion to animals today. Strange as it may sound, after we were left alone in that dreadful home, in many ways the dogs functioned as our parents. Not only did they protect us, but they also kept us warm at night and comforted us in our despair.

Occasionally we'd run out of food before our mother showed up again to replenish our supply. I'm sure she intended to come back to restock the cupboards, but then she'd get involved in her own life, and days would pass before she would show up again. Isn't it just amazing what you'll eat when you're hungry? When I became desperately hungry, I resorted to eating the dogs' food. On one occasion I can remember being so hungry that I actually resorted to gnawing on a dog's bone for nourishment. It felt so degrading to me to do this, but I had no choice. I was hungry.

Desperate for companionship, I remember calling those talk lines advertised on television. I recall that a man asked me inappropriate questions with sexual innuendoes during one of those phone calls. Of course I had no idea then what he meant.

As young as my sister and I were, we didn't have the know-how or the skills to keep house or cook food for ourselves. We had a roof over our heads, and the house was warm, and we had no chores.

There were advantages to living without adult supervision, and one of these was that we only had to bathe or brush our teeth when we felt like it. We never had to pick up our clothes or do the dishes or even clean up after the dogs. What kid wouldn't love this? In our minds this lack of rules was great, but then you have to live with the consequences if no one else is around to do it for you.

During the day while we were away at school, the dogs remained locked inside. By the time we returned home in the afternoon, the animals had destroyed the house and filled it with their waste. Instead of being greeted by the typical loving mom with milk and cookies, we were met with an awful stench of waste and urine. The inside of the house was revolting. Yet the dogs were so happy to see us that we would forget all about our surroundings. The dogs' warm welcome made us feel loved.

Although we missed a lot of days at school, I liked school because it not only allowed me to escape our living conditions every day but also provided the socialization I was lacking in my life. Children long for boundaries, and since we had none at home, school became the only place they were set forth for me. It felt safe.

Like the lines in one of my favorite books, *Sense and Sensibility*, when the two sisters argue, "You conceal nothing," my sister would complain. I would reply in continuance of Anne Austen's words, "You confide nothing and I am an open book." Often I'd gotten myself in trouble that way, but my sisters warned me never to say a word about our circumstances, so when a teacher would occasionally question me about my home life, I would stare blankly into space without revealing a thing.

Remnants of memories from Nana and Pop-Pop's home filled with love and order, and the aroma of tasty food, and crisply ironed clean clothes danced through my head as I lay with the dogs at night and cried myself to sleep. I would also think of my father. If only my father had remained in Colorado, he would have looked in on us just as Mordecai in biblical times looked in daily on his cousin Esther when she was living in the king's court. Mordecai was responsible for Esther and wanted to make sure she was safe. If only my dad had been there, he would not have turned a blind eye toward the situation, and how different our lives might have been.

It hurt to think of him so far away from us, living in Florida with his new family that he had recently begun to build with his wife Sharon. I assumed these new children had replaced us, that we were long forgotten. I believed we were to blame for wanting to move back to Colorado when he had given us such a nice home. In our minds there was no way for Kristine and me to go back to live with him since we'd burned our bridges.

Even if we'd been able to muster up our courage to ask him to allow us to move back in with him, we wouldn't have the opportunity to ask him since he wasn't around. I felt I was being punished. Was I being punished for choosing my mother over my father? This doubt that plagued me was the beginning of a long struggle for me to make decisions in my life.

Chapter 3

Cinderella

How much did I hear of religion as a child?
Very little, and yet my heart leaped when I heard the name of God.
I do believe that every soul has a tendency toward God.
—DOROTHY DAY, *The Long Loneliness*

S oon after Pop-Pop died and Mom left us in the house with the
dogs, she married her boyfriend John, and they were living in
a five-thousand-square-foot house on a golf course in Evergreen.
They were friends and neighbors of the prominent Hinckley
family, whose notorious son John attempted to murder President
Reagan, one of my favorite presidents. While we lived in sordid
surroundings, Mother and John were living in the lap of luxury
among the rich and famous.

On occasion they would allow my sisters and me to stay the
weekend at their home, and on Monday morning Mom would drive
us back to our school, which was over an hour away from their
home. We never understood why we weren't allowed to live with

her and John, and they never bothered to explain why. It was always a sad occasion for me when we had to leave Evergreen. As a child I naturally assumed it was because John didn't want to have kids around and have to share my mother with us.

Evergreen was a pristine little mountain town. When we visited, we had a wonderful time. We'd go to movies and do other fun stuff. We lived such parallel lives, for when we were with Mom and John, we were in a huge, beautifully decorated home, rode in John's big Cadillac, and had access to all the finer things in life. Then they'd take us back to the filthy doghouse. Not understanding my parents' flaws, I concluded something was wrong with me, something unlovable. Whenever someone would spend an extended period of time with me, it appeared to me that they eventually became tired of me. My motto became, to know me is to hate me.

My sisters and I were constantly struggling to figure out why my mother behaved as she did. From the time she was very young, my mother's beauty and seductiveness had attracted scores of men. She was one of those femme fatales who knew how to cast a spell over a man.

This type of woman is portrayed in novels, movies, and soap operas. Perhaps my observation of my mother is one of the things that fueled my career as an actress in soap operas. Typically the female villain in the soap operas will stop at nothing to get what she wants, and this was very familiar to me. My mother had many of the same characteristics as the women depicted in the soaps.

How did my mother become one of these women? Against her parents' wishes she had married my father when she was sixteen years old in an attempt to escape her difficult circumstances at home. When she was a child, her mother's constant criticism made her feel that she was a bad girl and unworthy of anything. Even more a detriment to her self-esteem was the fact that she didn't even finish high school because her children came immediately. By the time she was in her early twenties, she was an "old" married lady with three children.

Beginning to feel tied down and trapped, Mom probably felt cheated that she had forfeited her teenage years and became saddled with a husband and three small children, so she began to seek excitement elsewhere.

A local anchorman and celebrity, John had the money she needed to indulge in her love for animals. With John, the animals got bigger. Our father could afford her dogs, but John had enough money to buy horses for her. Apparently, my mother cast her spell over John; but unlike many of the other men in her life, his deep love for her had conditions. John would tolerate all of her shenanigans, except her children. Remember the old adage, children should be seen and not heard? John must have believed that children should be neither seen nor heard.

Once I mustered the courage to ask my mother why she was more concerned for the dogs than us. She reminded me that an animal cannot take care of itself and we could. I think my Nana said it best: "Most people carry around pictures of their kids, but your mom carries around pictures of her animals."

In a childlike way I tried to explain to my mother that we were unable to take care of ourselves, but my words fell on deaf ears since my mom was a real pro at denying reality. She successfully invalidated my feelings by telling me I was a bitch and ungrateful for feeling the way I felt.

Fortunately, our sister Robin knew our situation and would occasionally bring us food. A typical teenager who loved to party, Robin was motivated to come to our house because we had no adult supervision. She would straighten up the house and invite her friends over for a party or a visit. All the older kids who hung out there thought we were lucky not to have any parents around. Little did they know.

I will never forget one particularly chilling night when I was twelve years old and watching television in the living room while Kristine was safely ensconced in her room. Suddenly I looked up from the television to see one of Robin's friends, an eighteen-year-old boy, standing there. Tall, with curly hair, the boy began talking to me and finally sat down next to me to watch TV. Before I knew it, he had thrown me down on the floor and gotten on top of me, holding my hands similar to how a wrestler pins his opponent. Without speaking a word to me, the boy unzipped his pants, yanked my panties off, and tried to force himself inside of me. Breathing heavily, he tried again and again to force himself in me as I lay there in a daze.

I had no voice; I couldn't scream. Neither could I protest or move my feet to run away. I was paralyzed. After several attempts, the boy was fortunately unsuccessful. Suddenly we both heard someone coming. The perpetrator jumped up and zipped his pants. I watched him nonchalantly walk out of the room as though nothing had happened, but what he had done would change my life forever.

I had never been taught to call out to God, and I was clueless about who it was that protected me. Burying my face in the pillow that evening, I felt more hopeless and alone than I ever had before.

For years afterward I suffered terrible nightmares from both this sexual assault and the effect of being left in the house without adult supervision. I always lived in fear of this happening again. As the boy held my arms down, a nail in the carpet sliced my hand. I still bear the scar, which serves as a reminder of the hopelessness I felt as a child. For years after the traumatic event, I dreamed that I was in danger, but I couldn't get my mouth open to scream or move my feet to run away.

Kristine made friends with a girl at school who lived in our neighborhood. Her name was Tracy, and Kristine is still in touch with this special friend today. Courageously, Kristine eventually shared our living conditions with her friend. In turn, Tracy told her family. The family lived around the corner from us in a cul-de-sac. They were blue-collar workers who had a tiny pocketbook but big hearts.

Once the family learned of our predicament, they insisted that the two of us come for dinner at their house every single night. They'd often take us places with them so we weren't so isolated. This family was a godsend. They will always have a special place in my heart.

God also sent us another family during our ordeal when I became good friends with one of my classmates, Laura. Becoming acquainted with her family illustrated to me what a family could be. They had twin sons who were great looking, good athletes, and also strong Christians. My first introduction to Christianity through their lives made a deep impression on me. Their lifestyle reflected Christ in all the choices they made for their lives. They never witnessed directly to me but showed me God's love through their prayers and lives. Maybe they just didn't know how, or perhaps they were afraid to interfere in the lives of other people's children.

Because they talked about God all the time, I thought God sounded like a good friend, and I sure hoped that I would meet him some day. I had no concept of who God was, and no one bothered to tell me. If I was unworthy of my parents' love, how could I be loved by God? I will never forget their kindness and the love of Jesus Christ they demonstrated to me at a time when my life was pretty bleak.

After living in the house alone for several years, our living conditions suddenly improved. Mom was no longer raising Great Danes but horses and needed a place for her newly acquired animals, so she and our stepdad rented a five-acre horse property and moved us into the house on the property. Not only were my parents frequently at the horse property, but I also have some joyous memories of returning home from school and running into the barn to saddle up the horses to ride.

At the same time my older sister Robin moved back in with us, so the three of us lived at the rustic farm alone when our parents returned to their home in Evergreen. Our lives began to feel a bit more normal since Robin was older and knew how to manage things better than Kristine and I had alone.

A few months later my mother persuaded my stepfather to sell their luxurious home in Evergreen and buy her a forty-acre horse ranch in the town of Elizabeth. She convinced John that she could turn her passion for horses into a profit if she had a ranch.

By the time we moved into their new ranch, Robin had graduated from the infamous Columbine High School, was working and had her own place. We were hopeful that we might have more contact with Mom and John since they moved many of their possessions to the ranch. Our hope was short-lived when they informed us that they had also rented an apartment in downtown Denver where they planned to stay during the week so my stepfather John could be nearby the television station for the early morning news hour.

Even though it was just the two of us again, Kristine and I believed that at last we had a real home again. Before long though Camelot ceased to be. We soon realized that we had become prisoners on the forty-acre horse ranch, miles from nowhere. Especially since neither of us were old enough to drive. Along with caring for our two dogs, Kristine and I now had the thirty newly acquired horses to feed and care for daily. We cleaned stalls and performed other hard-labor chores. In the frigid Colorado wintertime, Kristine and I had to feed the horses and carry buckets of hot water to the horses when the water would freeze. We loved the horses and struggled to do our duties as best we could, but personally, I felt like Cinderella but with no hope of a Prince Charming coming to my rescue.

At different times our mom hired ranch hands to help around the property. Most of them were nice, but sometimes it felt creepy having them there on the property when our parents weren't around.

At ages fifteen and thirteen, Kristine and I were more mature and could take better care of ourselves; but our chores and school-work kept us busy from dawn until late at night. We were embarrashed to have our friends over because we still had the Great Danes who destroyed the house. In addition, we spent most of the time caring for the horses, and there was no time left to straighten the house. Nor did we have the know-how to do housework.

Author Christopher P. Johnson wrote, "An excellent woman who embraces her own domesticity also domesticates her children by training them. She teaches them how to do the domestic things, which she does and thus she prepares them for life."[2] We could not have been less prepared for life because our mother was not interested in housework herself, nor did she teach us how to do anything around the house. Still, there were positives in our lives. Mom was devoted to her horses so she was around much more often.

Once I expressed my frustration over all the work involved at the horse farm to my mother, but she turned it back on me, as she often did: "I'm doing this for you." Kristine and I loved the horses, so we didn't want to complain too much because we feared they'd be taken away from us too.

Like most children we craved the love and attention of our mother, and any time spent with her we cherished. A child doesn't know that her parents are unfit. Ironically, as a child you think you are the one who is unfit. Never does the thought occur to you until you are an adult that you are not to blame for neglect and abandonment. To us it didn't matter that she wasn't a typical mother; she was still our mother, and we loved her, and it was all we knew.

Clearly our relationship with her was strained. Although we were spending more time with our mother, most of her affection was lavished on the horses, not her daughters. I continued to feel unloved, worthless, and insignificant. Our stepfather made frequent visits to the farm, but he clearly wasn't enamored with the idea of having children around, so he remained distant. John was never abusive or mean to us, but a coldness exuded from him toward us. As my father had once been, my stepfather was under my mother's spell.

Was it because we were our father's children that caused my mother to reject us? Everything revolved around the horses and the dogs and their needs. My mom's obsession with the horses, as it had with dogs, spun wildly out of control. I felt like any value my sisters and I had to our mother had been based on what we could do for her horses and dogs. I was never valued for who I was but for the tasks I could perform. As a result, the animals became more important than the family in all our lives. It's no surprise that I have a passionate love for animals today, but I am able to keep my passion under a healthy control.

I will never forget the day my mother rescued an abused horse. Although the horse's behavior was undesirable, my mother had purchased the horse because of its great beauty. This said to me at a tender age, "If you are beautiful, it doesn't matter how you behave; you are forgiven of a multitude of sins."

If a man approached the wild animal, she would pin her ears back and jump violently in her stall. I intuitively sensed a deep hurt and rejection in the rambunctious horse. Looking back now, I believe the horse and I both must have sensed the pain in each other and immediately bonded, two neglected abused creatures with no one in the world to give us love.

Legendary horse trainer Buck Brannaman, the man who inspired Touchstone Pictures' movie, *The Horse Whisperer*, advocates trust not terror to turn a frightened horse into a friend. Totally unaware of his methods at the time, I instinctively used these same techniques to make this unruly horse that I named Chandy, my friend. For hours I would stand outside the horse's stall and coax and console her with my gentle words.

Later I learned that Brannaman, himself, was an abused child. In an interview he admitted that the same compassion and empathy he has brought to training disturbed horses helped him deal with a history of conflict and violence. This same technique also helped to heal me of a lot of hurt and rejection.

The horse community was amazed at how quickly I won the disturbed horse's trust. They were more amazed when I began riding her to the winner's circle at the horse shows. I spent long hours riding that horse. I would jump on her bareback and ride through the hills for hours and forget all the pain in my own life. A deep understanding and intimacy grew between us, horse and girl. We communicated through our broken hearts. One heart spoke to the other. I was able to give that horse the love I so desperately needed.

Chapter 4

School Days

Who would ever think that so much can go on in the soul of a young girl?
—ANNE FRANK, *The Diary of Anne Frank*

I n spite of her faults, our mother was a charismatic individual, and we all adored her, especially John. He often would reminisce about the first time he had seen her at the country music function. "Your mother was so beautiful with long red hair flowing down her back, and her lively spirit instantly captured my heart." When our stepfather didn't have obligations at the studio where he worked, he, too, was at the farm in a concerted effort to spend time with her. We were always competing with him for our mother's attention and affection. Having never had children of his own, he didn't know how to be a nurturing stepfather.

Whenever my mother was present, she was nurturing to everyone around her. I believe this nurturing quality of hers is what always made her absence seem so monumental in the hearts of my sisters and me. It was a big deal for us to have Mom and John around more often.

During this time I spent with my mother, I once came home from an acting seminar to find that she had written a note in my class workbook that I'd left lying around. It read: "Your mother loves you." I can't tell you how much it meant to me to read those four little words on that piece of paper. I have not only treasured them in my heart for years, but to this day the notebook where she wrote her declaration of love to me is among my most priceless possessions.

Because my mother couldn't express that she longed to be near us, I believed that her presence resulted solely from her wanting to be near her animals. I knew in her own way that she loved us, and I learned as an adult that her deep affection for the animals was rooted in her insecurity. Because animals won't abandon you or hurt you or betray you, they became a safe object for my mother's love. Animals are totally dependent on human beings, and that made my mother feel she had some power where the animals were concerned. Looking back to my childhood, I realize that my mother used animals to fill that God-shaped hole in her soul.

Having our mother and John around more frequently gave our lives more similarity to the lives that our classmates enjoyed. This was the life Kristine and I had so desperately wanted for many years. As a result, we developed a stronger sense of self and obtained an inner strength against the world.

This newfound strength was nothing to compare to having the Holy Spirit as I do today, but at the time it filled a portion of the gaping hole in my heart and soul. Having a bit more normal life with Mom and John resulted in my positive attitude about our new home and school. I had not experienced this feeling of hope since the day we left our grandparents' home.

When we lived alone, Kristine and I never found happiness or contentment at the schools we attended in the city. Our living conditions made it impossible for us to invite any friends into our home, so this prevented us from forming any serious relationships. Once we moved to the horse farm, we were optimistic that much of the social pretentiousness that existed in the city schools would no longer be an issue here in the country. This was true to a certain extent, but in spite of the lack of pretentiousness, our optimism was short-lived.

Nothing could have prepared us for the life we would soon endure at this small country school. We were immediately branded "new girls" at school. School had already begun when Kristine and I went to the counselor's office to register for our classes. Outside the counselor's door, several boys gathered in the hallway to peek inside the office. The counselor started laughing and explained that the boys were there to check out the new girls. Having so little self-esteem, Kristine and I weren't even sure what that meant, but we soon found out exactly what he meant.

The next morning the counselor warned us that those same peeping toms had promptly broken up with their girlfriends in hopes to vie for our affections. We were stunned, and apparently so were their girlfriends.

It was no surprise that my sister and I became instant enemies of the girls at this school. The resentment those girls felt toward us our first day of school grew with each passing day. It would follow us for years to come.

For the first time in my life, I suddenly became aware that I was pretty. Before, I'd always felt ugly and undesirable. For a teenage girl who had once believed she was invisible, this attention from the boys was flattering to me. Neither Kristine nor I knew how to handle our newly discovered power. Both of us felt self-conscious to be suddenly thrust in the spotlight. It became even more uncomfortable for us when those farm girls threatened to beat us up for this uninvited attention that we were getting. Both Kristine and I were scrawny little things, so we lived in fear of these daunting farm girls.

The situation grew worse when the senior girls cornered me one day at school. Sneering and jeering, they picked me up and dumped me into a trash can. While I struggled to wiggle out of there with no success, a large crowd gathered to laugh at me. I was humiliated, but I was stuck in that trash can, so I couldn't budge. At a point when I felt I could no longer bear the humiliation, one of the friendlier girls at the school, Sarah, came to my rescue. At that moment Sarah and I became instant, forever friends.

Although Sarah took a lot of grief from the other girls for befriending me, she ignored them. Sarah had gone to Elizabeth High School with these kids all of her life, and she was enormously popular. She could get away with it. She was the daughter of the town sheriff, which gave her a certain amount of clout. The kids at school found it advantageous to be Sarah's friend when they ran into trouble, which they often did.

Having Sarah as my friend was a blessing for me. She persuaded me to try out for cheerleader, and when we learned that we both made it, we were ecstatic. At Elizabeth High School we enjoyed many activities together, especially cheerleading. Had it not been for Sarah's encouragement, I would have never mustered the courage to try out for cheerleader. Having a good friend like Sarah was indeed a treasure that I had never experienced before, and her friendship became a positive influence in my life. She didn't care about my living conditions and didn't make me feel ashamed about how I lived. Coupled with having parents around for the first time in years, Sarah's friendship afforded me a new sense of security. Yet there still remained a hole deep in my soul.

It didn't matter to me how or with what I filled the hole in my soul. Like an indiscriminate scavenger, I was desperate to replace the emptiness with anything I could find—garbage in, garbage out. *Do not have other gods besides Me (Exod. 20:3)*. Not only did I break this commandment, but I would continue to disregard it for many years. I put everything before God because I had no knowledge of his existence. On my quest to fill the empty hole inside of me, I found many things to fill my empty soul, most of them destructive.

My people are destroyed for lack of knowledge (Hos. 4:6). I was afraid to admit there was a God because I feared he, like all the other authority figures in my life, would disappoint and hurt me. Worse yet, I was afraid I might disappoint him, and then he'd reject me forever and abandon me like everyone else in my life did.

The community we lived in was isolated, making it difficult for young people to socialize. There was no movie theater, no bowling alley, or even a youth center. Our activities centered on bonfires, four-wheelers, and tailgate parties. It was illegal to start these fires, and we mistakenly thought no one would know, but the smoke would rise high into the Colorado sky. Fortunately we had Sarah's father, the town cop, so we could talk our way out of any trouble.

Ultimately, all this time on the hands of the young people in the area proved that *idleness is the devil's workshop*. They spent most of their time involved in sex, drugs, and alcohol.

Through it all, I survived, but not before I learned one of life's important truths: beauty means power. When I discovered I was attractive to the opposite sex, I didn't know how to handle it. Only a short while ago, I had been traumatized over the attempted rape by an older guy, but when a young female is starving for male attention, she soon discovers a value in her sexuality.

I was desperate for the reassurance that I was lovable. I learned that even more power to attract love was attainable if I used my body since few teenage boys could resist the temptation. This was not real love, of course, but at the time I didn't know that.

At the tender age of fourteen, I unceremoniously lost my virginity to an eighteen-year-old boy at school whom I had dated for several months. At the recent Billy Graham Crusade in Los Angeles, Dr. Graham pointed out that the commandment, *Do not commit adultery (Exod. 20:14)*, encompasses all the sexual sins. Since this sin would include sex outside of marriage, I had just broken my second commandment, and it would not be the last to be broken.

I never felt as though I mattered to anybody, but I discovered that when I was about to engage in sex with a man, I now mattered! Although only for a few moments, when I was engaged in the sex act I had my partner's undivided attention, and nothing else in the world distracted or mattered to him but me. He didn't care if the phone rang or whatever because I became my partner's total focus. What power! What control! I'd never felt so important in all my life.

Now that I had tasted power, my appetite for sex became insatiable. But it was not because I enjoyed sex. In fact, I detested it. Today I realize that it wasn't a hunger for sex but that I was starved for the intimacy and attention that had been denied to me most of my young life. I quickly learned to control men with the use of my sexual power. I was like the guy who dumps the girl after sex. I became totally unattached in my relationships. This would be my weapon of choice for the next several years of my life.

Although most of my classmates were heavy drinkers and drug users, I rarely touched the stuff. No one forced me to try pot. But eventually I wanted desperately to fit in, so I tried it. Smoking pot made me feel cool, and it lessened my anxiety, so I figured it wasn't so bad. I soon found out differently. At sixteen, I smoked pot and drank tequila with a guy I had just met. Based on the way I felt, I couldn't help but wonder if my drink was laced with something. I couldn't move or speak but was fully aware that this guy was raping me. Losing control became such a frightening experience that

I vowed it would never happen again. After this incident, drugs and alcohol were no longer an option for me.

Many of the kids moved onto heavier drugs, but fortunately for me, I remained terrified of drug use. After a while, I longed to get away from these people and their destructive patterns centering on sex, alcohol, and drugs, but once again I saw no escape.

Rodeos proved to be the perfect diversion to me, incorporating all my favorite things—horses, country music, jeopardy, and of course, men in cowboy hats and tight-fitting Wranglers. Following the rodeo, people from all around would gather at the fairgrounds to listen to country music.

It was here that I was introduced to country dancing, and I immediately loved it. A friend of our family taught me how to dance, and it became, and remains today, one of the greatest passions in my life. While this escape was only in my mind, it would transport me to another place and would influence me for a lifetime.

Out on that dance floor I was nothing but a white-trash redneck, but I loved every minute of it. Like the tragic verses I could pen for a country song, "I didn't have anybody to love me, nor did I have a dime, but I could forget my troubles when I twirled around the dance floor in perfect time."

The country dancing I loved most was swing dancing and the Texas two-step. Since line dancing was solitary activity, I refused to participate in it because I never wanted to do anything alone. I craved the comfort of having another human being with me, close to me. Besides being fun, I found the intimacy of country dancing temporarily met my needs. The man's focus was totally on me when we were dancing.

In country dancing, unlike freestyle dancing, you and your partner are dependent on each other. You move in harmony. When dancing freestyle, partners don't even have to look at each other or pay any attention to the person they are dancing with, but when a couple is two-stepping, they are totally focused on one another.

There were flips and dips in the dancing, so I soon found I could literally lose myself in the steps and forget all my troubles. Invigorating, the dance steps and the music transported me to another world. The lyrics to the country songs were so heartfelt that it seemed as though the singers were my family. Through the words of their songs, the singers gave me advice and guidance. I learned more about life, love, and relationships from the western songs than anywhere else. Maybe this is why cheating on your lover appeared so normal to me, a part of life, since it was the central theme of a lot of country music back then.

Throughout my teen years, I tried to run from my pain and loneliness with men, country dancing, or horseback riding. I kept trying to find something to suppress my pain and loneliness. I thought if I could just keep moving, it wouldn't catch up with me, but denying reality doesn't change the circumstances. As much as I tried to act like they didn't exist, those feelings were coloring all my choices.

Had I only known then that there was a heavenly Father to take away my pain and sorrow, I could have escaped the suffering I endured for many years. *The Lord GOD will wipe away the tears from every face and remove His people's disgrace from the whole earth (Isa. 25:8).*

Another way to escape some of my difficulties was to work. To earn spending money, I worked part-time for a local tree company after school and in the summertime. One day when I had to go out to the tree lot with the owner of the company and my class-mate who also worked there, I was standing in the door of the truck reviewing some paperwork when I felt my boss walk up behind me. Before I could turn around, he pushed his body firmly into mine.

I was terrified, but once again I couldn't find my voice to scream. Besides, we were miles from nowhere. Who would hear me? My boss had sent the other boy deep into the woods. Fortunately, the boy suddenly reappeared to rescue me from this dirty old man. Even though I didn't know God, he always seemed to send an angel when I needed help.

In spite of my rescue, I wanted to get out of this community more than ever. I was determined to break the patterns I had established in this town and get a fresh new start somewhere else.

But the real catalist for me was when one of our classmates, Jeff, was severely injured while driving under the influence of alcohol. Jeff almost died as a result of the accident. Upon his release from the hospital, he looked a mess. His jaw remained wired shut, and he was ensconced in a halo apparatus.

Despite Jeff's condition, one night I was shocked when I saw him at a party drinking beer through a straw. This horrific sight proved to be an epiphany for me. It was the impetus I needed to get away from this school and these people.

A few days later my best friend Sarah came to pick me up for school, and I flatly told her I wasn't going to school. My mom was at the farm that day and asked me if I was ill. I told both her and Sarah, "No, I've made a decision. I'm not going back to that school."

Wide-eyed, Sarah tried to persuade me to go, but my mind was made up. I refused to go.

"But you can't quit school," Sarah replied.

I informed my mother and Sarah that I was going to quit that school, but I did have another plan. Another girlfriend, Holly, had recently transferred to Ponderosa High School just over the county line, and I told them I had decided that I was going to go there too.

"Then I'm going with you," Sarah replied. "I have a car, and I can pick you up and drive you to Ponderosa every day."

We talked to Holly, and she explained that if we knew any people who lived in the Ponderosa school district, we could use their address and enroll in the school. Who did I know who lived in the district?

Mom suggested we ask my Uncle Don who lived in the area, so she called him and got his permission to use his address. At the time no one gave me a lecture on truth. I had just broken another commandment. *Do not give false testimony against your neighbor (Exod. 20:16).*

A few days later I was the new kid in school once again when Sarah and I enrolled in Ponderosa High School. Instantly I loved it. It was big and brand-new. There was excitement in the halls that I had never felt before. On my first day at school, I got a lot of attention from the guys. As I had learned at Elizabeth High School, guys always like the new girl. I never felt that I was special; it was because I was new and different.

They had known the girls in the school for years through all the awkward stages of growing up—braces, pigtails, and acne; but now someone new and different was on the scene.

Even at this new, more sophisticated school, all the girls wanted to kick our butts for all their boyfriends' attention they thought we stole from them. But Sarah was tall and tough, so she stood up to them and defended both of us.

The decision to attend this school was a good one. I was having a wonderful high school experience. The education was far superior, and my grades improved drastically. Because this school was larger and offered many more activities for its students, I didn't get roped into following the crowd as I had at the smaller country school.

There were also many more courses of study and activities to participate in at the new school. Discovering drama was life changing for me. Sally Smith, a caring drama teacher, instilled the love of acting in me. Being involved in the theater gave me a sense of purpose, which I had never experienced before in my life.

During my sophomore year I was inspired to try out for the play *Grease*. I was nervous at the audition, but when I discovered that I was one of the finalists for the role of Sandy, I was ecstatic. I had seen the movie *Grease* and related to the character of Sandy, who, like me, was the new girl in school. Unlike me, she had won the hearts of not just the guys but the girls too. I longed to be like her. I became so excited and wanted the part so badly, but the drama teacher, Sally Smith, ultimately assigned the role to a senior.

I was disappointed, but unlike the other times in my life this teacher offered me an explanation of why I was rejected for the part. She explained that she gave the role to the senior girl since it was her last year in school and assured me that I was talented and would have plenty of other opportunities.

Miss Smith then assigned a part in the chorus of *Grease* to me. The fifties-style dancing was similar to the country swing dancing that I loved so much. During this time my stepfather John was hosting AM Colorado, and he arranged for me to meet a lot of famous actors. There was no doubt that I knew I wanted to be one too. I had a great time being in the chorus. I danced and sang all the numbers. I realized that I loved acting because it afforded me the opportunity to escape my own pain, to pretend that I was not myself. It also gave me the attention I desperately needed. For the moments I was up on that stage, I was someone else.

Throughout rehearsals the drama teacher encouraged me. Sally Smith created a nurturing environment in the drama department.

Not only did she make acting really cool, but also she encouraged her students to take risks, and she was supportive of all the students. She cared about her students, and she was the type of teacher who you could go if you ever had a problem.

Had I not had my drama classes, I probably would've left the school because my best friend Sarah decided to go back to Elizabeth since she'd grown up there and she missed her longtime friends. I was happy to stay even without my best friend since I was enjoying the theater.

Between my junior and senior years of high school, our drama teacher arranged a trip to London for the drama department so we could study the history and experience the theater. To my surprise, my parents agreed to pay for the trip. Before the deadline to register for the trip, I read about a summer program at the Denver Center for Performing Arts. I wanted to learn the craft more than I wanted to study the history of theater; and since it was the same price as the trip to Europe, my parents agreed to pay for the classes instead. They even gave me permission to stay at their apartment in Denver during the weeks of my classes.

I was so excited on the first day at the Performing Arts Center. I discovered that I was the youngest person in the class, but I was so eager to learn, I didn't feel intimidated at all. During the summer program I studied voice, stage combat, scene study, acting techniques, and stage movement. It brought my acting up to a higher level too.

Studying acting was something John could identify with, so during this time the two of us became closer. John interviewed a lot of celebrities on his talk show, and he invited me on the set to meet many of the actors. Observing all the attention they garnered, I knew I wanted to be an actor. I also got to spend more time with my mother that summer.

Best of all, the animals weren't around in the city, so I didn't have to compete with them for my mother's attention. Having access to both parents that summer helped me to grow and flourish in my acting, as well as in many other aspects in my life. I felt so mature and responsible going to this class every day.

At the end of the course, we presented a play at the Denver Center of Performing Arts. It was exciting because this was the stage that was used when all the big shows came to town. The name of our play was *The Art of Dining*. Being on stage was magical. I was hooked.

Returning to the ranch was a letdown, but I was looking forward to my senior year in high school, especially returning to my drama class to implement the techniques I'd learned in my summer program. When school opened in the fall, I learned that Miss Smith had left, and a new teacher, Kim Moore, was now head of the drama department. What a delight it was to discover that Mrs. Moore used a technique similar to what I had learned at the Denver Performing Arts Center over the summer.

During my senior year, I was driving to school on my own in a beat-up old GMC truck that we had on the farm. Most of the kids at the school were from affluent families, so what a contrast this old banged-up truck was sitting in the school parking lot amongst the BMWs, Mercedes, and other fancy cars. It didn't bother me one bit because I felt so fortunate to escape my reputation at the other school. At the new school I was into the whole country thing. This made me unique, and my classmates always noticed and admired anyone who was different.

My life had improved, and my future was looking so much brighter until my friend Holly and I were called into the office by the vice principal, who accused of us of crossing county lines to attend school. She informed us that we would no longer be able to attend the high school unless we lived in the Ponderosa school district.

By this time my sister Kristine and my friend Sarah had already graduated, and there was just no way I could face returning to the country school alone. The thought of the life I had led while going there repulsed me. Now what?

Chapter 5

A Place to
Hang My Hat

All I want is a room somewhere.
—Alan Jay Lerner, "Wouldn't It Be Loverly," *My Fair Lady*

Faced with the alternative of returning to the country school, I finally mustered the courage to pick up the phone to call my Uncle Don and Aunt Sheri to ask them if I could move in with them in order to qualify as a student in the school district. They said yes, and I was so excited. I had always liked my uncle and aunt.

I thought my Aunt Sheri was an amazing wife and mother, so cool, especially for an adult. I happily packed my things to move into their home in Parker, Colorado. I had a large room in the basement with my own bathroom in a nice home filled with love, laughter, and good food. It wasn't a fairy tale life because my uncle would sometimes leave while my aunt was at work and say he'd be right back. I'd get stuck babysitting and have to cancel my plans, but I made up my mind not to let other people get me down anymore. I accepted the fact that I had to earn my keep. I was a teenager now, and I knew everything. By now I had developed a thick skin that nothing could penetrate. I was determined that no one was going to hurt me anymore.

One of the things most teenagers take for granted is having a neat and clean house to bring their friends home for a visit. Because of the dogs, our home was always a source of embarrassment to me. Since moving from my grandparents' home at age ten, I had never had a home that was decent enough to invite guests over to play or for a visit. I would often go to great lengths to avoid allowing my friends or my dates to see inside my home. If someone came to pick me up, I would just pray that they wouldn't ask me to use the restroom. How exciting to live in a home where I could invite my friends to come over for a visit.

It took some adjusting to get used to having rules at my aunt and uncle's home. There had been so few in our home. Only once did I recall that my mother said I couldn't go out with a certain guy. Ironically, she was finally protecting me—what I wanted most—but I wouldn't let her. Here we go again, dishonoring my mother. Once you break one commandment, it just keeps getting easier and easier. The conscience becomes crippled, so instead of honoring her, I screamed at her, "Why should I listen to you when you leave me alone most of the time to do as I please?"

"Because I'm your mother," she replied.

"That is a title that you earn," I informed her bitterly.

My mother reached out to slap me in the face, but I blocked her hand. That was the only time she'd ever raised a hand to me.

At my aunt and uncle's home I was expected to abide by a curfew. At first I resisted until I considered how fortunate I was that someone wanted to know when I was coming home. Someone cared that I came home. What a difference this made in my life. For the first time since I had begun dating, I even stopped bouncing around from one boyfriend to the next. I realized my motivation for doing that was the extra attention I got when two guys were competing for you. That usually ended in more trouble than even I could take, so I decided that I would try the commitment thing, but I still had to keep a guy on simmer, and another on boil for fear of being alone.

At this time I had a serious boyfriend, Sam, who respected me and didn't attempt to have sex with me. Initially I was flattered, but down the road the fact that he didn't want sex from me made me feel totally worthless. Without sex I thought I had nothing to offer him. While Sam tried to get to know my heart and mind, I was constantly trying to distract him with my body.

Emotional intimacy was totally foreign to me, and truthfully it frightened me more than the intimacy of sex. If Sam really got to know me, I feared he would discover, like all the others had, my secret: I was no good. This was my greatest fear. To prevent this from happening, I pulled out all the stops to seduce him, but this young man refused to compromise his morals.

Looking back, I feel so ashamed that I was the serpent in his garden, enticing him to sin. Yet Sam was a confident teenage boy, and even though he had a girl so willing that she not only offered herself to him but also begged him to have sex with her, he refused to compromise his morals. He turned me down.

Since I was incapable of maintaining a healthy relationship with a healthy person, I ran away from Sam. While he wanted emotional intimacy, I couldn't give him that; all I had to offer was a physical intimacy.

My mother arranged for me to buy a car for $800 with the agreement that I would work part-time to make the payments. Sarah and I, along with our classmate Tony, got jobs at the local pizza parlor, Vito's, owned by the football coach at my school. This was the local hangout for a lot of the kids at school. I loved my job, and once I even delivered pizza to the home of Denver Broncos quarterback John Elway. I was a huge fan of the quarterback, and when he came to the door, I was star-struck and couldn't speak. This was one of the perks I enjoyed about my job; the other was the free pizza I could take home to share with the family.

At school I became the sports photographer on the school newspaper. I photographed all the sporting events and even became the statistician for the basketball team. I also continued to enjoy my participation with the drama department.

I tried out and was in all the plays we presented: *Hay Fever, The Good Doctor,* and *The Miracle Worker,* but my favorite was the role I played my senior year; I was Snow White in *Snow White and the Seven Dwarfs.* I had to dye my blonde hair black for the role, but even that didn't bother me. This is, until the hair dye washed out and turned my skin black for several days! I loved acting. It afforded me the opportunity to escape from my own life and be someone else. Our cast traveled around to all the elementary schools in the area and performed the play for the schoolchildren.

All eyes were focused on me. People sat quietly and listened to what I had to say, even if they weren't my own words. Right now I was not only getting the attention I craved but also applause. Never in my life had I felt so important. I was a star! The applause was like a drug to me, and I wanted more. I was hooked.

Living with my aunt and uncle, I led the life of a typical teenager the last year of school. After my boyfriend Rob, I played the field; but during my senior year, I had a serious boyfriend, Alan, a high school stud who was a starter on both the basketball and tennis teams and made All-State for both. Alan broke up with me, and to show him, I dated his best friend—all a part of my destructive pattern. When Alan discovered what I had done, he said in no uncertain terms that he was disgusted with me. This wasn't the reaction I had hoped for. But he taught me a big lesson. You don't degrade yourself to make somebody want you. My social life was in its usual shambles, but my academic life showed promise.

After speaking with the counselor at my school, I decided to apply to Carnegie Mellon. I made the choice of a school strictly by emotion. Ted Danson, my favorite actor at the time, went there, so I wanted to follow in his steps. The college was expensive, but I didn't think this would be a problem since my stepfather appeared to make a good living in broadcasting.

Although I had applied to several other colleges, I was anxiously waiting to hear from Carnegie Mellon College. When the letter from the college finally came, I read that I wasn't rejected, but I wasn't accepted either. Although my grades had improved at Ponderosa High School, the damage had been done to my GPA at the country school. At least the college had placed me on the wait list. Hope remained.

After my high school graduation, my Uncle Don and I were having so many disputes over my babysitting his children that I decided to leave Parker. I wanted to have a carefree summer before I left for college and had to buckle down at school. We parted on great terms, and I relayed my appreciation and gratitude to my aunt and uncle. I appreciated the time I'd spent in their home and look back on the time I spent with them as some of my happier days in high school.

I didn't want to go back to the horse ranch, so I decided to ask my grandmother, who had sold her home and was now living in an apartment in Aurora, if I might spend the summer with her. At this point my grandmother had somewhat recovered from the loss of my grandfather and my cousin Eric had moved into his own apartment. Just as mysteriously as she had disappeared from our lives, she had recently reappeared by showing up at family gatherings and even came to my high school graduation. She and Mom had gotten into an argument at my graduation over who should get the credit for my success.

My grandmother said she'd be delighted to have me move in with her. An added bonus of living with her in Aurora was that my friend Sarah also was living and working there. I looked forward to a fun-filled summer. Aurora was a much larger town than Parker, and it felt cool to live in the "big city."

When I called Sarah to tell her the news that I was living in Aurora, I was surprised when she asked me if I would like to have her job. A free spirit, Sarah explained that she was moving to Hawaii in search of adventure, but she didn't want to leave her wonderful boss without a receptionist. Although I was sad that Sarah was leaving, I needed a summer job, so she arranged the interview for me. I was hired for the position and went to work right away. I loved my job and made good money. My new boss really cared about his employees, and unlike most of the men in my life, his concern for me was never inappropriate.

On my way home from work one day, I stopped at a service station to buy gas, and ran into Bobby, a guy who'd also graduated from Ponderosa High School. He smiled and ambled over to my car to say hello. Bobby was a bodybuilder and had a great personality. What attracted me most to him was that he was older. I thought he had it all together. Since I was always falling apart, this aspect was an even stronger attraction for me. Was I ever wrong.

As we hung out at the pumps, I flirted shamelessly with him. He had finished high school five years before me, but I'd seen him with some of my friends around Parker for several years. We chatted amicably about our mutual friends. Just before we said good-bye, he asked for my number.

Bobby didn't waste any time. By the time I got home, he was already calling, and we went out right away. I believed that a guy who obsessed over you was obviously in love with you, so I ignored the danger signals. He was charming and attentive, and it wasn't long until we were a couple. We had the perfect summer romance.

As fall grew near, I remained on the wait list at Carnegie Mellon and had to choose another school. Having been accepted at Colorado State in Ft. Collins, I decided it would be a good alternative to Carnegie Mellon. Several of my classmates from Ponderosa High School were going there, and also I would only be an hour away from Bobby, so I enrolled there. Bob was supportive of my college career and assured me we could continue to see each other on weekends.

After reviewing the college catalog, I met with my advisor and told her I wanted to be an actor. She suggested I should also consider a "plan B" since so few people make it in Hollywood. Good advice. I told her I had also dreamed of being a lawyer, so she suggested that I major in sociology since it would provide a good background for both law and drama.

These two professions paralleled beautifully. Both a lawyer and an actor do a lot of research prior to their performances—one on the stage, the other in the courtroom. In addition, an actor must evoke emotion from his audience, just as a lawyer does from his audience, the jury. Thanks to my astute advisor, I had found the perfect major.

Wanting to experience college to the fullest, I signed up to live on campus in the dorm, but because I had waited for admittance to Carnegie Mellon, I hadn't pre-registered for a dorm at Colorado State University, and they weren't sure they could accommodate me.

Mom and John were also enthusiastic about my college career and insisted on accompanying me to the campus to register. While John had earned a college degree, no one else in my family had ever gone to college, so it was a big deal for my family for me to enroll in college.

On move-in day I was pretty nervous waiting to see if I would be assigned to a dorm. Because I had registered late, all the rooms were taken, and I was put on a wait list. While my mother, John, and I waited at the housing office, I was introduced to another student, Teresa, who was in the same predicament. I learned that the housing department had paired us as roommates if we were lucky enough to get a room.

As we chatted, Teresa and I realized we had a wide range of common interests including horses. She told me she had brought her horse with her and had him boarded nearby. Over the next several weeks, Teresa and I would become good friends. Even our registration delays turned out to be a blessing for us.

I was beginning to see how sometimes what seemed bad at the time got used for the good. This godly principle would prove true for me many times in the future. They assigned us a room in the senior dorm, which just happened to be the same building that housed the Colorado State football players. How fun was that for two freshmen girls?

My freshman year was all that I'd hoped college to be. Immediately, I was popular and became involved around the campus. I was elected to the judicial board. What a great way to prepare myself for a law career!

In order to serve, the members of the judicial committee were required to attend an orientation weekend to learn how to make fair decisions. One of the exercises we were asked to do in the training session was to take out a piece of paper and draw a picture of our dreams. I drew a line down the center of my paper and drew a family on one side. On the other side I drew a stage. The instructor informed me that I couldn't depict two dreams, but I told him that I wanted both and there was no way for me to choose. Growing up, I had longed for a traditional family, so I was not going to scratch it out on my paper, and I certainly wasn't going to erase my dreams of an acting career.

When I returned from orientation, I got involved in the theater on campus and signed up right away to audition for the first play of the season, *Guys and Dolls*. Scanning the list of roles the director had posted, I was pleased to discover that I had landed a part in the chorus. We began practice immediately, so much of my time was spent with the theater crowd.

At last I seemed to be going in the right direction. For the first time in a school environment, I felt that I belonged. I was dating Bobby, making friends, going to classes, and participating in campus functions—a typical college student. I was building a future for myself that no one could take away from me.

My optimism about my future soared until the day after class I came back to my dorm to discover an ominous pink slip taped to my door. Opening it, I was shocked to read that the second half of my tuition for the semester hadn't been paid. There had to be some mistake! My mother and John had been so supportive and pleased that I was going to college. I called my mother to tell her about the note. "I just walked in and there was a pink slip on my door saying that you guys haven't paid my tuition. Is this some mistake?"

"No," my mother said rather matter-of-factly. "We don't have the money."

I couldn't believe my ears. My mother and John lived a lavish lifestyle, and now she was telling me they didn't have money for my college tuition. I hadn't even finished my first semester at school, and now I was going to have to leave.

I was so angry I slammed down the phone and called Bobby. "My mom has gone and done it again. I should have known better with her history of letting me down. Every time I've put the past behind me and tried to believe I could count on her, she's let me down. Why do I keep putting myself in this position, allowing her to disappoint me? Why did I even bother to go to college?" I complained to Bobby.

Quickly explaining that she and John hadn't paid my tuition, nor were they going to, I told Bobby that I wouldn't even get credit for the courses I had completed if this tuition was not paid. I learned to play up my disappointments from my family to get love and sympathy from Bobby. It worked like a charm.

I expected sympathy, and I got it. Bobby loved to rescue me. To my surprise he generously offered to lend the money to me so I could finish the semester. What a great guy! Not surprisingly there was a hefty price to pay.

What most girls like me don't realize is that these *nice* guys aren't necessarily nice, but they obligate you to get what they want. I was much too naive to recognize this at the time. Bobby also loved to attend all my pity parties and always reinforced how badly my mother treated me. This is just another control factor that these manipulative guys use to create a world of isolation for the person they love. In an effort to make a woman dependent on him and to him alone, they create a world where the object of their affection has no one to turn to but them.

I learned later that my mother and John really were having financial problems but at the time, I didn't believe her when she said they didn't have the money. I would not have drawn the conclusion that she didn't care about me; I would have surmised that she felt my future not worthy of her investment. She and John paid thousands of dollars for our horses to be trained by the top trainers in the country so that the animals had more value, yet their child got no money for training. Was I less valuable then the horses?

Once the semester ended, I got a job. I figured I could go back to college if I worked and saved some money. I never did, but even today my dreams of obtaining a degree are still alive.

Moving out of the dorm should have been traumatic for me, but a few weeks before I'd really blown my relationship with my college roommate and not being able to grasp the forgiveness concept at this time in my life, I couldn't wait to get out of there. I had wronged my roommate and felt I couldn't face her.

When Teresa went for a visit to her parents' home in Utah, she asked me to drive her to the airport in her car. Her car was much nicer than mine, and it was also full of gas. I was tempted. She would never know if I drove her car while she was away. *Do not give false testimony against your neighbor (Exod. 20:16).* Breaking this commandment became a habit for me.

After becoming a Christian, I saw all the ways that my heavenly Father was teaching me little lessons along the path that eventually led to him. *The LORD disciplines the one He loves, just as a father, the son he delights in (Prov. 3:12).* This was one time I had to suffer the consequences of my actions, and it was humiliating.

While Teresa was away, I was speeding down the street in the turn lane when a car pulled across and hit me. Fortunately, the accident was not my fault, but just the same, my roommate would know I betrayed her because the whole front end of her car was smashed. I was terrified. How would I ever face her again?

I couldn't face Teresa. I felt so terrible about the car accident that I convinced my sister Kristine to pick her up at the airport to tell her. I didn't have the courage to tell my roommate what I'd done to her car. When Teresa returned to the dorm, she was understandably furious with me. Once again I had proved to myself that I was no good.

Throughout my childhood I'd developed a way to deal with confrontation, and that was to withdraw. I think part of my shame was that she was such a sweet girl with unbelievable morals. Although Teresa told me she forgave me, I had no understanding of the concept of forgiveness, and I slithered away like a snake out of her life forever.

I planned to move back in with my grandmother, but Bobby insisted that I live with him. How could I say no? After all, he had paid my tuition. Bobby also made me feel like I was number one in his life. He gave me the gift that no one else did—time. My decision to move in with Bobby upset my grandmother terribly, and we had a big blow-up, which I deeply regretted because she'd been so kind to me over the past summer. Yet I felt obligated and succumbed to Bobby's pressure.

Believing Bobby was controlling, no one in my family approved of him. For the first time in my life, having someone to control me was such a welcome change after being on my own for most of my life. I felt secure that someone was looking out for my interests.

When someone has control, they also have responsibility, and that was comforting for me. I was trying to be a submissive woman, but I didn't have the knowledge that God wanted me to submit to a holy union and a godly man. Being submissive without those necessary ingredients is a risky business. Longing for boundaries, I sought out controlling men.

Chapter 6

Deadly Decisions

There can be no happiness if the things we believe in
are different from the things we do.

—Freya Stark, *The Lycian Shore*

After my brief college career ended, I moved back to Aurora
and got a job as a bank teller at First Bank of Colorado. Even
though this wasn't my dream job, I felt proud to have such a
respectable position at such a young age.

Although we never spoke of making our relationship official,
Bobby and I lived together. We said, "Why bother to get married?
It's only a piece of paper." The Hollywood couples were doing it,
and that made living together supercool. The Jon Bon Jovi song
"Living in Sin" was the hit tune blaring on the radio. It must be OK.
I was living by the world's standards and not the Word's standards.

Bobby had a good job in the high-tech industry, and now that
I was earning money, we both worked hard, played hard, and
partied hard. We pretended to be something we weren't. His boss

would often lend us his Corvette, and we would spin around town like two big shots. I was living that parallel life again, showing off in a fancy car just to go home to a room we rented in someone's house. I was working a full-time job and earning money to spend as I pleased. I had even managed to pay Bob back for the tuition he loaned me. This financial security offered me a sense of freedom I'd never experienced before. It also allowed me to buy my first new car, a Honda CRX.

Having someone to care about me as Bobby did gave me the feeling of having a father. I now had a man to do all the things that a father was supposed to do. It felt empowering. Within a year our utopia ended when I discovered I was pregnant.

When I told Bobby I was pregnant, he assured me it was not a problem, that I could easily get an abortion. I'd already told my mother I was pregnant, and she had rushed over with a baby outfit. Seeing that I was torn with this enormous decision, Bobby came up with the best argument for his case. He reminded me that he was a bodybuilder and was taking a heavy dose of steroids. "The baby is going to be deformed," he reasoned. These few words were all I needed to hear to justify the procedure.

Right away, over my mother's protests, I made arrangements at an abortion clinic. By now I was feeling all the effects of being pregnant. The emotions, the nausea, and the exhaustion made me feel like I had a bad case of the stomach flu. To me, an abortion was merely a cure for the flu.

I felt miserable, and to make matters worse, Bobby admitted that he didn't have the money to pay for the abortion. Although Bobby had a great job when I first met him, it wasn't long until I realized he had trouble keeping a job for any length of time. An entrepreneur, who was always chasing some get-rich-quick scheme, was telling me he had no money? Realizing that I would have to pay for the abortion myself, I felt angry.

Once again, the person I loved the most and the one I had given the gift of trust was saying, "You are on your own, baby."

The next day when I went into the clinic for the abortion procedure, I was bombarded with posters of aborted babies carried by well-intentioned pro-lifers. These people were trying to show me the seriousness of what I was about to do. But there was no way I would go back on my word to Bobby. My allegiance was clear; I wanted to please him, not the protesters, not God, or myself, and definitely not my mother. *Honor your father and your mother (Exod. 20:12)*. I failed miserably at this commandment.

I followed the nurse back to the surgical room like a robot. The uncomfortable procedure was over in a few minutes. Problem solved. The doctor and his nurses performed their task like factory workers, moving from one patient to the next. No one offered any condolences. It was more like, "OK, you did great!" All I got was a pat on the back. How tragic that one of the few times I managed to get a pat on the back was for killing my baby. The nurse instructed me to get dressed, handed me the aftercare instructions and a prescription, and then sent me home.

Aside from a little cramping, I felt much better. Life could go on as normal as though the baby never existed. Now I had broken my third commandment, *Do not murder (Exod. 20:13)*. I had no idea how this would effect me until years later when I became a Christian.

We stopped by the drugstore on our way home, and Bobby offered to go in and get the prescription filled. I couldn't believe that he asked me for money to pay for it, as if my paying for the abortion wasn't enough. You would think Bobby would at least pay for the antibiotics. I dug what money I had out of my purse and handed it to him.

A few days later I woke up in the middle of the night in terrible pain. I was so restless and in such pain that Bobby complained that

I was disturbing his sleep. Clearly irritated, he reminded me that he had to work the next morning.

I got out of bed to go sleep on the couch so as not to disturb his sleep, but when I got into the living room, the pain had become so intense that I began punching the wall. Suddenly a big wave of nausea rolled over me, and I began to throw up. I couldn't stop. By morning, the pain became so severe that I called my mother.

Although my mother had encouraged me to have the baby, she was supportive of my ultimate decision to have the abortion. Alarmed by my phone call, she came rushing over to our apartment. When I answered the door, I was surprised to see her standing there, smiling and holding a bag from Taco Bell.

"You're upset and you're taking medicine, and if I know you, you haven't eaten," she tried to explain my pain away to soothe me. "After you eat this, I'm sure you'll feel better."

Everyone knew that a burrito supreme from Taco Bell was my favorite food. Mom expected the burrito would make me feel better. To her surprise, the sight and smell of the burrito caused me to throw up again. Placing her hand on my forehead, my mother with a look of concern also noted I was burning up with fever.

Realizing just how ill I was, she sprung into action. She always shined in these situations. Without hesitating, my mother telephoned our longtime family doctor, Dr. Arnold Tanis. "Bud" as we called him, was my pediatrician in Florida. After she explained my symptoms to him, he advised her to rush me to the emergency room.

Even after my mother's years of neglect, she could always be counted on in a major disaster. This time my mother saved my life.

At the hospital I learned that my insurance was lapsing for non-payment. Mom got on the phone with the insurance company and discovered that a payment had to be put in the mail today to prevent the policy from lapsing. She rang up my uncle Don, and he took care of it immediately so they would admit me to the hospital. Our family could always unite in a crisis. As dysfunctional as we all were, we really did love one another. I remember feeling more loved that day than at any other time in my life. A deadly seed was planted that you had to suffer in order to get attention.

Finally, the nurse took me back to the examining room where they began running a battery of tests on me. With a concerned look on his face, the doctor told my mother and me that his diagnosis was peritonitis, a life-threatening inflammation in the inner wall of the abdomen and pelvis—a result of an infection. He explained that they had to rush me into surgery immediately.

The nurse pushed a form under my nose while the doctor explained that the surgery was extremely serious. "Tracy, we'll do all we can to save your reproductive organs, but first and foremost, we have to save your life." The doctor shook his head and continued, "It may not be possible to save your reproductive organs, so it's going to be necessary for you to sign this release form for us in case we have to remove them."

I knew I had no choice. I had to sign the release form, so I took a deep breath and signed my name on the dotted line.

As they wheeled me down the long hallway strapped to a gurney and into the operating room, I remember looking back at my mother's face filled with concern. How good it felt to know that she was there for me and that she cared. The last thing I remembered was the mask they placed over my face.

Awakening from surgery in the recovery room, I saw Bobby, my mom, and the doctor at my side, and I heard the sounds of machines humming and beeping. I felt so much pain below my waistline that I felt as though I'd been sawed into two pieces. I looked down to see that my stomach was distended. I was terrified. I had just had an abortion, and now I looked more pregnant than ever.

Suddenly recalling the form I had signed I blurted out to Bobby, my mom, and the doctor, "Will I still be able to have children?"

Bobby turned red, so I naturally thought the news was bad; but when the doctor smiled a big toothy grin, my heart leapt. He announced, "The surgery was a success. We didn't have to perform a hysterectomy. You're going to be fine, Tracy."

I was so relieved. Before the doctor left, he paused at the door and turned around to scold me. "Next time, remember to take your medicine, Tracy. This could have all been avoided if you'd taken the full prescription of antibiotics."

"But I took them all." I explained.

"That's not what your mom told me." The doctor then nodded toward Bobby, then walked out and closed the door.

Confused, I looked over at my mother. She explained that when Dr. Travis, our family doctor, inquired about the meds that had been prescribed for me following the abortion, she consulted Bobby. Glaring at Bobby across the hospital room, she said he was defiant and didn't want to tell her at first, but she persisted. "Bobby, why don't you tell Tracy what you did?"

Sheepishly, Bobby had to admit to me that he hadn't wanted to spend the money, so he asked for only half the prescription. "I'm sorry, Tracy. I had no idea it would cause such a problem."

I couldn't believe my ears. I buried my head in my pillow. I thought Bobby was by my side for love, but he was there out of guilt. He knew all along! I'd been through all this because Bobby was too cheap to spend the money on my medicine. He had so little value for me that he didn't even spend the money to purchase the medicine I needed. I was furious with him.

Although my organs were not damaged, the infection was so advanced I had to be hospitalized for five days on I.V. antibiotics. Even the antibiotics running into my arm made me feel as though I had fire, not medicine, dripping into my veins. That's how potent they were.

When the nurse came in to check on me she asked, "How are you doing, Tracy? Are the meds burning you?"

"Definitely," I replied. "They're killing me."

"Why didn't you ring for me?"

"I'm not about to complain," I explained to her. "I deserve this pain and a lot more for what I've done."

All my troubles just came tumbling out of my mouth. I confessed that I had an abortion. "God is punishing me," I stated stoically.

The nurse gently patted my arm and consoled me. "Honey, God's already forgiven you for that abortion. Now you must forgive yourself."

I smiled at her. Her words were so sweet but it was merely a cliché to me at the time. I didn't have the capacity to understand what forgiveness truly meant.

After returning home Bobby and I fought continuously. I deeply resented him for the abortion and for the infection. During a heated argument I stormed out and went for a drive in my little Honda CRX, "the silver bullet." After driving around for an hour and listening to music, I stopped to get a soda at the convenience store located near the Arapahoe Community Airport, a small airport for private planes. I went up to the counter to pay for my soda and discovered that I didn't have any cash on me, so I whipped out my checkbook to write a check. Five guys came up behind me to purchase beer and offered to pay for my soda.

We started talking, and I decided they were a nice group of guys. I was so angry with Bobby that I was feeling rebellious. When one of the guys said, "We've chartered a plane to go up to Vail. Why don't you come along with us?" I thought to myself, *These guys are at least ten years older than me.*

The others chimed in with persuasion, and in my defiant mood, I didn't hesitate. "Sure," I accepted. I, like many girls, was easily flattered.

Once on the plane I realized what I had done. Nobody had any idea where I was. I pulled the pilot aside and spoke with him privately. "I don't know these guys, but I was impulsive and accepted their spur-of-the-moment invitation to Vail. Do you think I could fly back with you?"

He gave me his word that he'd take good care of me.

Fortunately, my traveling companions turned out to be nice guys. All we did on the flight was play poker and drink beer. They thought it was really cool that they had persuaded such a cute young thing to fly to Vail with them.

When we landed in Vail, I got off the plane and told the guys I was going to return to Denver with the pilot. Naturally, they begged me to stay. Ordinarily, I was so easily persuaded, but the pilot had taken such a fatherly responsibility for me that I stuck to my guns. The pilot reaffirmed I was going back with him. Truthfully, I was surprised when I boarded the plane to return to Denver. I couldn't have done it without the pilot. God provided an angel for me.

On the flight home we ran into a storm. There was lightning all around us. Sensing my uneasiness and fear, the pilot tried to distract me.

The pilot told me to put my hand on the windshield of the plane. When I did, electrical sparks came from my hand. "Cool," I observed. "That's St. Elmo's fire," the pilot explained.

When I looked at him quizzically, he explained. "St. Elmo's fire is an electrical discharge on a pointed object such as a mast of a ship or the wing of an airplane in an electrical storm."

I began thinking of how much St. Elmo's fire was like my life. Everything I touched sparked and burned and ultimately turned to ashes.

When we finally landed in Denver, I thanked the pilot profusely, then got into my car and drove back home to Bobby as though nothing had ever happened. At dinner that night he asked me, "What did you do today?"

"Not much," I replied, barely able to keep a straight face. I didn't dare tell him of my big adventure. All I wanted to do was please Bobby.

That all changed about five months later when my monthly credit card bill arrived in the mail. Opening it, I was stunned to see numerous charges that I hadn't made. My account was over the limit. It was obvious to me that someone had stolen my credit card, and after reviewing the familiar charges, I knew exactly who it was! I was livid when I noted that even the flowers Bobby had recently given me were actually charged to me.

Confronting Bobby when he arrived home, I called him a thief and accused him of stealing from me. After a heated argument, he finally admitted that he had used my credit card number. Bobby was a master manipulator. He tried to convince me that what he'd done wasn't a big deal. He turned it around like he always would and made me the bad guy. "What is your problem? Why are you so selfish?" Bobby asked.

He accussed me of having money issues. He tried to justify his theft, but when he saw that this wasn't going to work, he changed his tactic and tried to elicit my sympathy. "I love you so much that I just wanted to get those flowers for you so badly. I just wasn't thinking. My stupid company messed up and cancelled my credit card, and I didn't know what to do." Excuses, excuses! At this point in our relationship, I had sympathy fatigue. It was always something, and I was sick of it. He begged me to forgive him, but I had finally reached my limit.

I was wise enough to know that Bobby would never change, so if I didn't want to live like this any longer, I had to get out of there. When he left to return to work, I ran into our bedroom and packed up my stuff and loaded my possessions into my Honda CRX. My mind was made up, and I was going to get away from Bobby once and for all, even if I had to sneak away. I scribbled a note to him that read, "Sorry, it's better this way."

Chapter 7

Tracy's Big Adventure

It will never rain roses: to have more roses we must plant more trees.
—George Eliot, *The Spanish Gypsy*

Bobby didn't believe I'd do it, but I did it. I ran away from him. I drove to the bank to tell my employers I was resigning and moving to California to become an actress. Although I could tell they had their doubts about me, they wished me well.

I drove over to Nana's house to tell her good-bye and see how she was doing since breaking her ankle. When I told her I was moving to California to pursue acting, she said, "Yes I know" very matter of factly. I had always talked about it, but still never had. Nana knew a person is defined by what they do, not by what they say. She couldn't hear what I was saying because who I was, was speaking too loudly.

"No, I mean it. I'm leaving right now."

"Good," she said, "but you're not going to drive to California by yourself. Give me twenty minutes, and I'll go with you."

I was flabbergasted but delighted that Nana was coming with me. Nana had often shared stories of her life with me, but I couldn't believe she was still as spontaneous in her old age as she had been in her youth. Sure enough, in twenty minutes she came out hobbling on that broken ankle with her suitcase in hand, and we were off to California in my little Honda CRX! Nana had to stick her cast out the window in order to keep her broken ankle elevated.

It was getting late and Nana tried to persuade me to stop for the night in Grand Junction, Colorado, but I refused. I knew it was only geography, but just the same, I had to cross that state line.

"Nana, I have to get out of this state," I explained. "If I don't, I'm afraid Bob will somehow find me and persuade me to come back."

She understood my concern. Once we crossed the state line and reached Green River, Utah, just over the Colorado border, we pulled into a little motel for the night, and Nana insisted on paying. We were both exhausted and exhilarated at the same time. Before we went to bed, I called my older sister Robin who had recently married and moved to California, to let her know we were on our way.

The next day we drove until we reached my sister Robin's home. Since it was Halloween, we had to dodge the trick-or-treaters as we drove into her driveway.

Robin was happy to see us and hugged us. She explained that her in-laws, whom I'd met and liked from a previous visit, had offered me free room and board in their home. Sadie and Charles Kerry were a nice couple; he was a successful psychiatrist, and she was a housewife. They had a large home with a pool and a full-time housekeeper.

After I got my grandmother on a plane to go back to Colorado, I settled into my new home. Immediately, I got in touch with a couple of my high school friends who had moved to L.A. to pursue their acting careers after high school. They were delighted to hear from me and warned me of all the pitfalls of becoming an actor. Their warnings didn't scare me in the least. I knew it wasn't going to be easy, but I felt encouraged because if anyone could handle rejection and disappointment, I could.

After I'd lived there for several weeks, Dr. Kerry came into my room one night when his wife Sadie was out of town.

"What are you doing?"

"Watching *Cheers*." I laughed because everyone knew I never missed my favorite TV show.

"Mind if I watch with you?" He asked.

"No, of course not." I replied. Even though I really didn't feel comfortable with him in there, it was his house, so I was polite.

To my surprise, instead of taking the chair beside my bed, he climbed into the bed with me and got under the covers.

"Tracy," he said. "I'm here for you if you ever need to talk."

"OK," I said matter-of-factly.

Then Charles took his glasses off, and I said, "Can you still see the TV without your glasses?"

"No, but I can see you." To my horror, he reached over and tried to kiss me.

Appalled, I jumped out of bed and asked, "What do you think you're doing?"

"Nothing, forget about it," he replied. To my relief he climbed out of the bed and left.

Why does this keep happening to me? Why can't I ever find a safe place to live? I grabbed my bag, packed a few of my things, and ran from the house. I got into my car and drove away. Where would I go? Not to Robin's house because I was afraid to tell her what her father-in-law had done to me. The knowledge would complicate her life beyond measure.

Whom should I call? I decided to call my girlfriend Suzy. Following our high school graduation, she had moved out to California to pursue acting. Previously, I'd called her a few times, the first time to let her know I was in town. I stopped at a pay phone and called Suzy to explain my situation to her, and she gave me directions to her house.

Still fairly new to California, I got back on the freeway and exited at the wrong ramp. Before I knew it, I was terribly lost and unfortunately at the time, I didn't have a cell phone. There was no way I could call Suzy until I found another phone booth. Circling the blocks, I couldn't find one.

When I finally found a convenience store, I pulled into the parking lot to ask for directions and saw two guys in a Mercedes. I asked them for directions to Suzy's house. They smiled at each other and said, "We'll do better than that. Follow us, and we'll take you there."

These good Samaritans led me right to my girlfriend's front door. When Suzy came to the door, she was shocked when I introduced her to my new friends. After the guys left, Suzy looked at me incredulously and lectured me, "Tracy, do you have any idea what you just did? They could have led you any-where. You can't just trust everybody."

I realized that these two guys could have knocked me in the head and I would have never been seen or heard from again, but for some reason I totally trusted them. Were they angels that God sent to me to help me find my way? I had to sleep on Suzy's hard floor that night, but at least I was safe.

The next day I called my sister Robin. I decided to go ahead and tell her what had transpired at her in-laws' home. Expecting sympathy from her, I was shocked when she reprimanded me.

"How dare you be rude to my father-in-law? You were totally out of line, Tracy. Charles was just trying to help you, and you took it the wrong way. They were doing you a favor by letting you stay with them."

At that moment I realized there was no one I could really count on but myself. I felt betrayed but I also knew that it was impossible for her to take my side. Growing up we had learned survival of the fittest.

Robin subsequently invited me to her house to do my laundry every week. She would send me home with clean clothes and hot food. Although very grateful, I wanted her loyalty. I wanted to be defended and protected.

When something frightening happens to a young girl, she instinctively runs into the protective arms of her father. Since I had no earthly father I could count on nor did I know a heavenly Father, I had no one to fill that hole in my heart and soul. Typically I gravitated to the current man in my life. Since I was alone at the time, I thought of the last man in my lifeBobby. I had come to California to escape him but it was only geography.

By now I was feeling a bit guilty anyway over what I had done to him, so I picked up the phone and called him.

Bobby didn't react with any anger over how I had left. Instead he focused on my vulnerability, which was always his way into my life. Although my sister hadn't come to my defense, Bobby quickly rescued me like a knight in shining armor. Within moments, he was back in my life.

Bobby flew me out to Colorado so we could be together again. He surprised me with a romantic weekend at Beaver Creek Ski Resort. When we rode the ski lift to the top of the mountain, to my surprise, Bob took a beautiful ring he had designed for me out of his pocket and proposed to me.

I had to pause to consider how I should respond. My responses in relationships were based more on obligation than on my feelings. When someone said, "Thank you," I said, "You're welcome." When someone said, "I love you," I said, "I love you too." When someone said, "Will you marry me?" I'd say, "Yes, I'll marry you."

I thought I should feel grateful that someone wanted to marry me, but since I was not in touch with my feelings, I hadn't considered whether I even wanted to marry Bobby. All I had for reference were the wildly romantic movie scene where the girl jumps up and down and cries tears of joy and says yes. The tears wouldn't come, nor could I muster up the enthusiasm to jump up and down, but I did manage to say yes. It was like a reflex.

I was like a closed piano without any notes. I couldn't open my heart to play a melody of happiness because I feared the notes of sadness would pour out of me instead. I couldn't think of anything else to say to this man who had just asked me to become his wife.

Bobby said he had no problem with my living in L.A. He supported my career and told me that he wanted me to succeed. He announced that he had a new job and was being transferred to Phoenix, Arizona. Since this move would shorten the distance between us, our problem was temporarily solved. We would commute and spend our weekends together.

Bobby also promised me that he would eventually move to California. Back then I thought it was because he loved me so much. Later I learned it was because he was a con man who had already burned his bridges in Colorado. He was moving to Arizona to attack a totally new market of suckers. I think he figured he would work over Arizona and leave his victims in the wake, then he'd be ready to marry and move to uncover a whole new territory of suckers in California.

At the time it appeared to me that Bobby was really trying to accommodate the desires of my heart. I began to feel more positive about accepting his ring and decided to call my family. At this point in my life, I was estranged from my mom and John and my sisters, but I called them and my grandmother to share the news of my engagement. Unanimously, they did not hide their disappointment.

Upset that I had regressed back into a relationship with Bobby, they were furious to hear I was now engaged to him. They strongly voiced their concerns over Bobby's manipulative control over me.

I went back to California and showed off my ring to Suzy and her roommate. Finally someone was happy for me. Everything was going well again, even though I was sleeping on Suzy's floor. In a few weeks I landed a job working at HWE, a company that made massage products for *The Sharper Image*.

At first, getting to work was a challenge and driving in L.A. was daunting. Going to and from work, I would go opposite routes to avoid having to make any left-hand turns. Somehow I found a meandering route to my office.

After a few weeks at work, I got to know my coworkers, Cindy McDonald and Tony McWilliams, the administrative assistant to the president. We became instant friends. Cindy was appalled to learn that I was sleeping on the floor at my friend's apartment. When she had begun to work at HWE, she had rented a room from Tony, so she suggested that I ask her if I might do the same. Upon my request, Tony offered me a bedroom in her luurious town home near the office. I jumped at the chance to rent another place for the exact rent I was paying to sleep on the floor.

I treasured the friendships with my coworkers but my relationship with Bobby drove my best friend Cindy crazy. She found him obnoxious and abusive. Like my family, Cindy could say or do nothing that would sway me. It appeared that the more people voiced their dislike of Bobby, the more obligated I felt to stay with him. I felt this insatiable need to defend him. *Poor Bobby, the poor baby is so misunderstood.* Why couldn't they see the side of him that I loved? The truth was, they saw what I was too blind to see.

I just forged right ahead with this dysfunctional relationship. Bob rarely visited California. If I wanted to be with him, I had to drive to Arizona. Almost every weekend I'd make the six-hour trek to Arizona. I often persuaded Cindy to come along with me. Once out of L.A., we'd speed down the long stretch of the 10 Freeway to Arizona, talking and laughing all the way. Passing through Blythe one weekend, we were pulled over by a cop. When the police officer came to the window, he said, "Tracy?"

I said, "Rick?"

Cindy said, "You guys know each other?"

"Yes," I said. The same cop had pulled me over once before on this route.

I was shocked when the cop told me that he hadn't stopped me for speeding at all. He explained that because they had spotted my car going up and down the highway so many times that they suspected I was making drug runs. I couldn't believe it.

Rick and his partner searched the car until Cindy and I finally convinced him I was just another lovesick female chasing a man. Of course, no drugs were found.

I worked at HWE close to a year until I decided that if I was going to pursue acting I needed a job with more flexible hours. The time had come to focus on my career. I resigned from HWE and found a more flexible job teaching aerobics at the Holiday Health Spa.

Chapter 8

Stars in My Eyes

Hollywood's a place
where they'll pay you a thousand dollars for a kiss
and fifty cents for your soul.
—Marilyn Monroe quoted in *Popcorn in Paradise*

I had flexible hours at the health club where I worked, but the real benefit of the job was that I got in amazing shape. I'd never looked better in my life. Members at the health club often asked me if I was a model. I was flattered by all this attention. One of the members was convinced that I should be modeling and gave me a list of agents.

I called them all, but only one agent, Irena Kamal, set up a meeting with me. A longtime modeling agent for the Playboy Modeling Agency, Irena had recently decided to branch out on her own. The meeting was going well, but when she learned I didn't have a portfolio of modeling photos, she turned me down immediately.

"Wait a minute. You just said you liked my look. I can get a portfolio, but someone with a portfolio can't get my look," I responded boldly.

I must have convinced her because Irena looked me straight in the eye and said, "OK, I'll represent you."

"You won't be sorry," I replied and thanked her profusely.

I wasn't an overnight success, but I got a few little jobs, which helped me pay off some of my bills. Irena often teased me after an audition, "Sorry, Tracy, you didn't get the job. The breasts beat you out again." *Baywatch's* Pamela Anderson and former playmate Rebecca Ferrari were my competition, and I wasn't in their league. Having large breasts appeared to be a must for most of the models hired by Irena's clients. I quickly learned that making it in Hollywood without large breasts was definitely against the odds.

Without an ample chest, I felt pressured. I eventually acquiesced and had cosmetic surgery of my own. Years later I realize what a mistake this was. Today as a Christian, I know that my beauty, even with its imperfections and shortcomings, is a gift from God. The writer of 1 Peter says it best: *Your beauty should not consist of outward things [like] elaborate hairstyles and the wearing of gold ornaments or fine clothes; instead [it should consist of] the hidden person of the heart with the imperishable quality of a gentle and quiet spirit, which is very valuable in God's eyes (3:3–4).* At the time my mother begged me not to have the breast augmentation, but her request only made me want to do it more. Why did I continue to sin and dishonor my mother? Maybe because I like to refer to my twenties as the "terrible twos."

A girl's got to do what a girl's got to do, or at least what she thinks she's got to do. And this girl was not going to allow anything or anyone stand in the way of what she wanted. I was trying to force my own will for my life.

Initially Bobby didn't appear eager to move to L.A., but it didn't matter to me. I had grown to like the long distance thing. He was like a toy on a shelf that I could go see when I wanted, but was still there to catch me when I'd fall.

Just as I was feeling comfortable at being on my on, Bobby decided to move to L.A. With Bobby moving, living with Tony was no longer an option. I now had money, and it was time for me to make a move.

House hunting was fun, and I was so excited when I found an adorable guesthouse in Burbank. It was furnished, and from the minute I saw it, I knew it was the home for me. My landlords were wonderful people who made me feel very welcome. They were always concerned about me but never interfering in my business. It was an exciting time for me. I had a real place to call home that belonged to me, and no one could take it away from me!

Bobby made plans to move to L.A. and began shipping a lot of his things to my place, but since he hadn't committed to a moving date, I continued to make the long drive to Arizona on the weekends.

One weekend when Cindy accompanied me to Arizona, Bobby left to go on a business appointment. Cindy and I puttered around the house doing domestic stuff. After folding his laundry, I was putting it away in his drawer when I discovered a card from a girl.

I couldn't resist the temptation, so I read it. To my dismay, it was an intimate note brimming with juicy details of the sender's relationship with Bobby. It became obvious to both Cindy and me that Bobby and the author of this note were more than friends.

I became irate. Cindy advised me to take the card and place the ring on top of it and to leave it on the kitchen table. "That will say everything." She explained. "Let's get out of here."

I loved Cindy's poetic advice, but I didn't have the strength to practice it. "I've got to talk to Bob first. I've got to know what's going on," I whined.

"What could be plainer than this note?" Cindy demanded to know as she waved it in the air under my nose.

For a few moments I considered what Cindy was saying, but I didn't want any good sound advice. I didn't want to do what was right. Like my abortion I only wanted something to make me feel better instantly. "I can't break up with Bobby," I told her. "He's moving into the guesthouse with me in a few weeks. He's already shipped half his belongings to California."

"You mean to tell me you can't break up with him because he's already gone to the trouble of shipping some of his things to your place? Ever heard of UPS?"

I knew what Cindy was saying was true. The evidence was there, but I refused to believe it, mainly because I didn't want to lose Bobby. Even though people everywhere were validating me for my work in commercials, I still had a strong need to have a man in my life, and to not be rejected or abandoned even if it meant forcing something that I should let go.

When Bobby returned, I confronted him. He told me all the lies I longed to hear. Cindy stood by and rolled her eyes in my direction.

Days later, when Cindy and I returned to L.A. I admitted that I was still infuriated by my discovery.

Being the good detective that I was, I located the woman's phone number and called her. I impulsively concocted a terrible scheme. "Hello, this is Dr. Hall, and I'm trying to contact Miss Smith."

"This is she," the woman said.

"Miss Smith, I'm afraid I have some rather disturbing news. I've called to inform you that Bobby Moore's tests came back positive."

"What tests?" the girl asked, her voice wavering with alot of concern.

"I'm afraid that's a private matter, but Mr. Moore listed you as one of his sexual partners. I need to ask you a few questions about your level of intimacy. Have you had unprotected sex with Mr. Moore?"

"Yes."

"OK, Miss Smith. I'm not allowed to discuss this over the phone, but you must make an appointment with your doctor right away. Good-bye."

I knew for a fact that Bobby had lied and cheated. I guess I was looking for a way out of this relationship.

I called Bobby and told him what I had done. "I never want to see you again," I screamed.

But like many times before, he convinced me not to break up with him. I welcomed Bobby back into my heart and my life.

Bobby knew he had put it off long enough and he moved into the guesthouse with me. My landlords discreetly asked me what I was doing with that con man. Like so many others, my landlords were not pleased. They took an instant dislike to Bobby. While their opinion embarassed me and made me feel ashamed, it did not disway me.

With all this chaos in my life, it was no wonder that my work had slacked off. I had recently resigned from teaching aerobics at the Holiday Spa and had gotten a great new job to supplement my income. I worked for a man whose company made soup bases for restaurant. My boss had a beautiful home in Marina del Rey over-looking the ocean. His office was in his home, so I was able to enjoy all the luxuries of his successful life, plus he allowed me time off to go out on auditions.

In addition to my exceptional work environment, my new boss was a generous man who paid me extremely well. Happily married, my boss had a stunning wife, and they had a loving marriage.

After working there a few weeks, I grew envious of this couple and all their many blessings. *Do not covet your neighbor's house. Do not covet your neighbor's wife (Exod. 20:17).* Not only did I covet his house and his money, but I also coveted the life this man's wife had with him. Her husband absolutely adored her and was devoted to her. This man was a good provider for his family. This was something I'd always longed for throughout my life. Why couldn't I attract a man like this who would give me love and all these other things? I became consumed with envy.

Curious to discover more about these perfect people, I decided to sneak a peek at their lives. I slipped up to their bedroom while they were away, and I opened a drawer and read all the cards he had written her. Next I examined the items on her vanity. Perusing the beauty products she used, I longed to emulate her. I was obsessed with this couple and all they had, especially their seemingly perfect life. Casing their home like a burglar, I noticed a jar of coins. *They'd never miss a few coins.* Just as I was helping myself to some money, he and his wife walked in and caught me red-handed. This was it. I was not only fired; I had also broken another commandment: *Do not steal (Exod. 20:15).* My life was going downhill quickly.

Next my landlords, the Bergs, politely took me aside and told me that the garage apartment was set up for one person, so I would have to find another place to live since my boyfriend had moved in with me. I blew something good for having my loyalties in the wrong place.

Bobby and I moved out and rented a townhouse in Burbank. I kept going out on auditions for the agency and continued to book a few small jobs. Irena announced that she hired a new agent who handled auditions for commercials. I was so excited to have a new opportunity to try out for television commercials.

Instantly I experienced success. Irena called me with my first commercial offer, but then she surprised me and told me she had received simultaneous offers for me to do two national ads, but unfortunately they were both shooting the same day so I had to choose one of them. This is such a Hollywood dilemma, feast or famine. No one wants you until someone else wants you.

The first offer called for me to do swing dancing for a Tecati Beer ad in Mexico, and the other was a stunt double to ride a horse for an Old Spice commercial in the USA. How cool was that? I was being asked to do acting that involved both swing dancing and horseback riding, the two great passions of my life. Could it get any better than this?

My agent expertly advised me to take the Old Spice commercial because it would qualify me to join the union. Becoming a union member is a huge obstacle for all actors, so there was no question; I chose the Old Spice ad. Although I was only a stunt double, I could hardly wait to report to my first union commercial job. A stunt double is hired for the principal to do the things the principal cannot do, such as in this case, to ride a horse bareback alongside the water's edge.

The decision to take the Old Spice commercial turned out to be fortuitous. The commercial was filmed in Bodega Bay along the Northern California coast above San Francisco. What made my first shoot even more exciting was that this was the exact location where Alfred Hitchcock had filmed his horror film, *The Birds*.

On the first day of the shoot, a beautiful girl sitting next to me introduced herself. "Hi, I'm Tiffany."

"I'm Tracy. I'm the stunt double."

"I'm the talent," the woman responded proudly.

"This is my first commercial, but I have had a lot of experience with horses."

"Oh, that's good because I've only taken a couple of riding lessons." She covered up her lack of equestrian experience by regaling me with stories of her success as a commercial actress. "I've worked a lot this year. Why, I even bought a Mercedes with cash," she boasted, "and I'm married to a psychiatrist."

"That's great," I replied, pretending to be happy for her, but truthfully since I was still struggling to pay off my ancient little Honda CRX, I must admit that her revelations stung me a bit. OK, a lot—I was green with envy! I wanted a Mercedes. Oh, and a rich husband too! Another commandment broken again, *Do not covet (Exod. 20:17).* I was relieved when our journey ended and we reached the beach, our destination.

The assistant director greeted us at the site of the commercial and led us over to the location trailer where an Apache Indian suddenly appeared and introduced himself. "Hi, I'm Cochise, the makeup man." He was warm and flamboyant, and I liked him immediately. I recognized his great sense of humor when someone stuck her head inside the door of the trailer and asked him for a can of hair spray. "First they take our land, then our hair spray," he complained.

Everyone laughed. Cochise, the makeup artist, looked at me and then the other actress and said, "Tracy, why don't you have a seat in the chair?"

"You don't have to do me," I explained. "I'm the stunt double so no one will see my face."

"I'm the talent," the pretty actress spoke up as she plopped herself down in one of the makeup chairs.

Cochise looked at the talent then back at me. Without a word he excused himself and went outside to talk to the director.

When he returned, he told the principal to go to the set because they were ready to do some set-up shots.

In a few minutes the director came into the trailer. "Tracy, can you come out here and see if you can get that horse to run?"

The makeup artist gave him an "I told you so" look and ordered me to get out there. When I stepped out to the beach, the talent was pulling back the horses' reins and kicking him at the same time. No wonder the horse wouldn't budge. That horse was reacting the same way that I did to most of the circumstances in my life. I always wanted to get moving, but my fear, like the reins on the horse, pulled me back. Ironically, the only place I didn't fear was atop a horse.

For a few minutes I stood back to give the actress another chance to get the horse moving. I watched her struggle until the animal finally took a few slow steps.

The director instructed the talent to get down and asked me, "Tracy, see if you can make that horse run."

It was now my time to shine. Someone offered to give me a leg up.

"A real cowgirl doesn't need a leg up," I boasted as I grabbed the horse by his mane and swung up on him. Everyone was awed by my show-stopping performance. Now the director instructed me to run the horse as the camera drove along beside me. Believing the horse wouldn't run, everyone was caught off guard when the horse and I took off like a bullet.

The director began chasing me down the beach, yelling, "Whoa, Tracy, slow down!" The horse, which had not run for the talent, was now racing down the water's edge with me, the stunt double on his back. Now that they had their set-up shot, they told me I could return to the trailer.

Cochise was waiting for me. Once again he told me to sit down.

I reiterated, "I don't need makeup. Have you forgotten? I'm the stunt double."

Cochise grinned and explained, "They're going to use you as the principal, so we won't need a stunt double. They're sending the other actress home." I ran to the window of the trailer and saw that the other actress was already in the van that was pulling away from the set.

I just stood there in a daze and asked, "What?"

"You've got the part!"

I was trying to be cool, so I resisted jumping for joy, but inside every part of me was screaming hurray! I couldn't believe my good fortune.

Cochise wondered why anyone would want to try to match the actress with a stunt double who was equally as beautiful and could ride a horse too. I had Cochise to thank for my job, as well as the horse that wouldn't go.

After Cochise did my makeup and I was fitted into my costume, I went outside to await my instructions.

Just as I stepped outside on the beach, a frigid gust of October wind whipped all around me, causing me to shiver. At that moment I learned just how special it was to be an actor. Before you even have an opportunity to get the words out your mouth to ask for something, there is always someone on the set who has already anticipated your need. Wow! Unlike my childhood where my needs were not always met, this business with all its perks was seductive for me. This time the person waiting to attend to my every whim was the prop man. He rushed over and placed a heater at my feet—instant warmth. I gave him a big smile. "Thank you. I'm Tracy."

"Bob Feffer," the friendly man replied as he shook my hand firmly.

For a moment there was only silence between us; then Bob complimented me. "I saw you on that horse out there. Pretty impressive."

"You like horses?"

"I sure do. I'm considering buying a horse." Bob Feffer grinned at me, and then we began a conversation about our mutual love of horses and didn't stop talking until the director called me to step in front of the camera.

"My family has some horses for sale," I added.

Bob seemed interested, so before I said good-bye, I gave him my phone number.

Then I went out and jumped on that horse and rode like the wind.

The Old Spice ad was a huge success. Overnight I felt I had earned the approval and acceptance of everyone. My confidence soared. For the first time in my life I had a voice. Ironically, it wasn't my voice but the voices of the characters I played.

In some ways my success doing the commercials was daunting to me, but I loved every minute of the work and adulation. Before I knew it, I had booked several national commercials for the Olympics, Coca-Cola, and Taco Bell. At twenty-two years old, I suddenly found myself earning over $60,000 a year. Now my fiancé Bobby was beginning to feel like an albatross. My thoughts were on the prop master I'd met on location.

Bob Feffer and I made a definite connection in Bodega Bay, so I wasn't surprised when he called me right away. I kept his phone calls a secret from my fiancé. Since they were both named Bob, I called my new friend Mr. Feffer. My fiancé had no idea I was cultivating this friendship with another man behind his back.

There was nothing illicit about my phone calls to Bob, but I knew it was devious on my part since I was engaged and living with Bobby. Mostly Bob Feffer and I talked about horses. When he told me he was serious about buying a horse, I put him in touch with my mother right away.

Previously my mother had stubbornly refused to sell any of her horses, but since my stepfather had recently retired, coupled with her poor business practices, their circumstances had changed drastically. Since Bob was my friend, my mother was open to selling him one of her horses, and she suggested that he come to Colorado to see them.

Unbeknownst to my fiancé, Bob Feffer subsequently made arrangements for the two of us to fly to Colorado. When we arrived at the stable where the horses were boarded, Bob immediately fell in love with Conrad, a beautiful animal, who was a half-Arabian paynt. Not only did he buy the horse, but this kind and generous man, out of the goodness of his heart, also gave my struggling parents some extra money.

I had a great reunion with my horse Chandy while we visited my parents' ranch. When Bob saw me with the horse, he was duly impressed, especially when I told him that she had once been an abused horse. I explained how through my patience and love for the horse, I'd won the animal's trust. I told him how Chandy and I had developed an understanding of each other. The pain of the abuse we had both suffered in earlier years was lessened as a result of the close relationship between the horse and me as a young girl.

"That horse belongs with you," Bob surmised. I was thrilled when he announced that he would pay to bring Chandy out with his horse, Conrad.

Having my horse Chandy in California with me strengthened me in many ways. At twelve years old I had loved her back to life, and in return she had given me life. When I began riding again, that life took on much more meaning than ever before. I spent every spare moment riding her. Going out to the stables and talking to Bob, I grew closer to him. It was only natural that he started hearing about my relationship with Bobby.

"Does this Bobby have a job?"

"He's not working regularly." I admitted. "I'm supporting him." The more I talked, the more I suddenly realized that my fiancé had no respect for me, and I certainly had none for him. The truth is that we both cheated on each other with other people. The only difference was that he'd been caught cheating; I hadn't. I was far too embarrassed to admit this to Bob Feffer, but I felt exhilarated playing on his sympathy. He was hanging on to my every word. I was playing the part of a damsel in distress, waiting for him to rescue me.

Bob scratched his head, as he always did when he was thinking, and then offered me a room in his house. He arranged for me to have my things moved out of the house I rented with my fiancé.

Of course it wasn't long until my friendship with Bob Feffer crossed the line to romance. Still craving a father, I discovered him to be the perfect father figure for me.

I'd grown up believing that I had to earn my keep, and Bob did take care of all my needs, so I was more than willing to move in with him. After all, he had a beautiful home and gave me all the money I wanted to spend.

Bob was always accessible and available since his profession allowed him so much freedom. He was always ready to go wherever I wanted to go and do whatever I wanted to do. Having never been around a generous man before, I was overwhelmed by his gifts to me.

Through the association with my family, Bob's interest in horses grew. When my sister Kristine called to say she was going to attend an Arabian horse show in Scottsdale, Arizona, we decided to meet her there. During our trip, we were saddened when Kristine shared her present living circumstances with us.

Recently the bank had foreclosed on my parents' horse ranch, and Kristine confessed that she and my mother were forced to live in an old camping trailer. Since the trailer was so small, there was no room for our stepfather John, and Kristine told us that he was actually living in his car. I couldn't believe it!

Oh, how the mighty have fallen! Tragically, John had gone from being a successful news broadcaster for a national network affiliate, and having his own celebrity talk show, to living as a homeless man.

Over the past few years, everything in my mother and John's lives had centered on the needs of the horses. It took an enormous amount of money to support the horse ranch, and my mother had flatly refused to sell any of the horses in order to turn the farm into a profitable venture. Previously, one of the horses my mother bred became a multinational champion, and someone made a lucrative six-figure offer for the animal, but she refused to sell her. Ultimately, she wasn't able to pay the trainer, so the courts demanded that the animal be sold at a Sotheby's Auction House to pay off the debt. Wayne Newton purchased the horse for his daughter at the auction. This was one of many of my mother's bad decisions that were based on her irrational fear that she was the only person in the world who could properly care for the horses.

My mother kept repeating these same old financial mistakes. As a result, she acquired thirty horses. She kept buying more and more horses to fill the void in her heart, but sadly, she remained empty inside. I think John must have figured, "Why work?" The more he made, the more she spent. In fairness to my mother, John allowed it.

I felt compassion for my family. I knew that Mom and John were responsible for their actions, but my sister Kristine shouldn't have to suffer. I asked Bob if Kristine could move in with us. I gave him an incentive to say yes by convincing him that Kristine could not only take care of the horses, but she could also break his

Arabian horse, Conrad, to ride. Bob readily agreed, so I invited Kristine to come and live with us. She decided not to go back home but to come with us to California.

Like many people, Kristine came to this great state and never left. She was free from my mother and the animals at last. I was excited to have my sister move in with Bob and me. Bob had his room, I had mine, and Kristine moved into the other spare bedroom.

Bob would do anything for me, and I slowly began to see many similarities between our relationship and Mom and John's. Was I really using Bob as my mom used John? Kristine was a welcome distraction from my concerns. She was excited about living in California, and I was excited about showing her around. We had never lived together under such great circumstances and luxurious surroundings, so it was fun and exciting. Just as we had done in our teen years, the two of us began to frequent the country bars.

For the most part, all the folks who go to these country bars usually aren't there for the drinking, but they truly love to dance and are great fans of country music. Country dancing is like a sport; you participate by dancing with everyone.

Since I was a relationship addict, it wasn't long until I met someone who intrigued me. His name was Randy.

When another patron told me that Randy danced regularly at this club, I insisted on going there every week. Randy was a marvelous dancer, and he really knew a lot about country music too. His dance card was always full, but that didn't stop me.

Kristine and I were having the time of our lives. It didn't take long for Bob to suspect that there was more going on in these outings than me and my sister going out to kick up our heels. Frequently, Kristine would come home hours before me, so he confronted me one evening. He told me he felt used and rightly so. He didn't charge me any rent and bought me everything I ever even mentioned that I wanted. He then confessed to me that he was hopeful that he and I might become more serious.

Since Bob had been so good to me, I felt terribly guilty, but I had to admit that I was falling for Randy in a big way. I knew that I needed to move out of Bob's house but when I told him, I could see the disappointment on his face.

Bob welcomed my sister Kristine to stay on since the arrangement with her training his horse was working out so well. She was grateful for the free room and board. Once I moved out of Bob's house, he began taking more and more out-of-town jobs. However, the two of them did develop a friendship that still remains strong to this day.

I suspected that Bob wanted Kristine to remain in his house so he could stay connected to me. I later learned that he had carried the hope that we would one day get back together and make our relationship permanent. Bob Feffer became the guy I always kept on the back burner. Like the Toby Keith song, "Who's Your Daddy?" I knew I could always fall back on Bob.

At the time I hadn't realized how much it appeared that I had used Bob. It had never been my intention to use him or to hurt him, but I was addicted to falling in love. Bob didn't deserve this for all the kindness he had bestowed upon my family, but I was a fickle and confused young girl. I always had to have one man on boil and another one on simmer.

Not many words passed between Bob and me as I began to pack my things to move out of his house. Bob agreed that I should move out. Yet instead of throwing me out to fend for myself, he helped me find a place of my own.

I had become an elusive butterfly flitting in and out of other people's lives without a thought that I was destroying them. I flew away from Bob into Randy's waiting arms.

Chapter 9

Wedding Bells

✳

Oh let us be married! Too long we have tarried:
But what shall we do for a ring?

—EDWARD LEER

I moved into a charming guesthouse in West Van Nuys near the 405 Freeway and Victory Drive, and it was a perfect for me. Working successfully in commercials, I could easily afford a nice lifestyle. Randy and I were free to date. At twenty-four years old, he was still living at home and making only seven dollars an hour as a maintenance worker at Park LaBrea. This didn't dissuade me one bit. I was now in the power seat. I was no longer the damsel in distress. I was looking for someone to rescue rather than someone to rescue me.

Previously in my relationships with both Bobby and Bob, I'd freely given them the power and control over my life. Bobby had put me down, making me feel unworthy. He cleverly kept me in this position by isolating me from my family and friends. Bob

Feffer had all the power because I was reliant on him financially. Like a father figure, he was always around to clean up my messes. Feeling like a child and not a girlfriend, I rebelled. By this time I'd learned that I wanted to be the one with the power so I emulated the two Bobs and took the power seat in my relationship with Randy. Finally I was with someone I could control. I was a modern, liberated woman who had it all figured out, or so I thought.

Besides, I saw potential in Randy. He was an excellent carpenter, so I used my connections to get him a job as a set builder making $28 an hour. I also loved the fact that he could fix things and do just about anything he wanted with his hands. He was also closer to my age unlike the older guys I had previously dated.

For most girls it would have been a major turnoff to learn that Randy still lived at home with his mom and stepdad. When he took me home for the first time to meet his parents, Mary and Ken, I clearly understood why he didn't wanted to leave home. Randy's parents were an amazing couple. Ken was an engineer, and Mary was a management consultant. They drove nice cars, lived in a beautiful home in the San Fernando Valley, and owned a beach house in Ventura County.

I suspect now that I was equally attracted to Randy's family and their lifestyle as I was to Randy. I believed if I married Randy, he and I would have the same life his parents were living.

Another source of my attraction to Randy was that he was enormously popular with all the ladies at the country bar, and I felt as though I had captured the prize. Randy was one of the greatest dancers I'd ever met, and the female in couple dances is only as good as her partner. Dancing was so important to me that I figured that by marrying Randy I'd never want for a dance partner to twirl me across the dance floor again.

Best of all, from the moment we met, Randy made feel me like I was number one in his life. He was in love with me, and it was so sweet and innocent. I was his hero. He said that he felt I was out of his league. This was great news to me because I figured he would never hurt me or leave me. Within weeks he proposed to me.

Most girls would have been thrilled at the proposal, but I felt like, *Oh, no, here we go again. Why do guys feel they have to mark their territory.* I knew in my heart that I could play the seduction game and get men to fall for me, but how long could I keep up the act? Truthfully, I didn't want to get married, but if he wanted me, who was I to say no? I'd been conditioned to be a sweet, agreeable girl, and I played the part well. I just wanted to be loved. Being engaged had its advantages, as would marriage. I believed it would give me respectability. Of course, I was wrong.

Surprised to hear the news of my engagement, my family and friends were curious and asked, "Who is this guy?"

Did I have the heart to tell Bob Feffer I was engaged after all he had done for me? A few months before, he had rescued me from my engargement with Bobby, and now I was engaged to another guy.

Randy and I set the date. In thirteen months we would become man and wife. This gave me plenty of time to plan the perfect wedding. The wedding plans would distract me from the reality that I was incapable of real love. Because I felt so unlovable, I detested myself and couldn't respect anyone who loved me. I took the focus off the relationship and put it into planning a big party.

Randy's mother, Mary, was fond of me. Overjoyed that her son was going to marry me, she offered to pay for the wedding. Since my mother and John were in such dire financial straits and living far away in Colorado, I accepted her generous offer but I insisted on paying for my wedding gown. Naturally, she wanted her son to have a beautiful wedding, so she happily assumed the role of mother-of-the bride in addition to her mother-of-the-groom role, and helped me plan all the details.

We hired a country deejay so we could have country dancing at our wedding reception. Since this was the passion that Randy and I shared and what had brought us together, I planned our entire wedding around the country western theme. Randy and I decided to be married at the Calamigos Ranch in Malibu. It was the perfect setting for a country-style wedding. The planning was about to begin.

My mother didn't find it easy to stand on the sidelines during these planning stages of the wedding. It wasn't that I intentionally ignored my mother, but I purposely kept her at a distance to shield myself from another disappointment. At the time it was just a painful reality for both my mother and me that she wasn't there for another special event in my life.

Mary gave me the things my mother never could, both her time and resources. Unlike my mother, who poured all her time and money into her animals, Mary was devoted to her children. She had worked hard to provide for them, and because I was marrying her son, I also reaped the benefits of the many sacrifices she had made on their behalf. Instead of sharing these special wedding moments with my mother, I shared them with my future mother-in-law.

Reacting with anger, my mother told me how upset she was that I had shut her out of my wedding plans. Naturally, she directed some of her anger at Mary. Knowing some of the disappointments of my childhood, Mary felt compelled to step into Mom's role.

I resented my mom's jealousy over Mary. I had always felt that my mother only wanted to be there for the fun stuff involving her children. Never there to help me with my homework, she'd show up in the front row to celebrate my graduation. She was not there to teach me what marriage is supposed to be. Nor had she been an example of what God intended the wife's role to be in marriage. Yet now she wanted to show up for my wedding day wearing the mother-of-the-bride hat and a brilliant smile and to sit on the front row.

Trying not to be affected by my mother's protests, Mary and I kept planning the wedding. When we were going over all the details, my future mother-in-law asked me who I wanted to give me away. This single question triggered a myriad of emotions inside of me. My relationship with Mom and John was strained, so I immediately thought of my dad.

At this point in my life, I felt a deep longing for my father. I'd only seen him twice in the past fifteen years. Although he had been absent from my life for so long, when I called to tell him of my impending marriage, he quickly gained my sympathy. He explained how he desperately longed to be with his girls, but my mother had manipulated the situation to prevent it. Now that I was older and my mom's character had been brought into question in several circumstances, I sided with my father.

Because of his absence, my dad had the distinct advantage of being idolized in my mind as the perfect father. For years I had fantasized about him as a dad. He definitely had the advantage because he was never around to shatter this illusion of him I had created.

Another reason I wanted to ask my dad to give me away was that at sixteen I had legally changed my name to my stepfather John's last name, Lindsey. I chose John's name for a variety of reasons. I never liked my surname, Ort, and thought it unattractive, especially compared to my stepfather's surname, Lindsey. I'm sure the fact that John was a celebrity and that I wanted to have the same name as my mother also played a factor in my name change. However, at the time, my decision had devastated my poor father.

I wanted to make amends with my father, and how better to do that than to ask him to give me away?

When I informed my mother and stepfather of my decision, they were furious. I found it ironic that they would put up such a fight to walk me down the aisle when they would never fight for me as a child who needed someone to defend, protect, console, and nurture me.

It appeared to me that my mother and father were competing for my loyalties. I was the rope in their tug-of-war. When I chose Dad, it marked the first time he'd ever won.

Not only was my mother livid that I had chosen my dad over John to give me away at the wedding, but she also set out to mar my happiness with guilt. "John assumed he would be giving you away and has already rented his tuxedo," she informed me. She succeeded, for I became riddled in guilt.

Over the next few days the situation escalated. My mother was now enraged. She threatened not to come to my wedding. I could no longer base my decisions on the fear of her response. While I wanted my mother and John to come to my wedding, a part of me didn't really care. I had gotten to the point where I wasn't angry or hurt with my parents anymore. I just wanted to get off the merry-go-round with them, so I became indifferent.

Although I was unaware of it, in denying John the honor to walk me down the aisle, I was able to express my anger at him for what I had perceived as taking my mother from me.

In retrospect, I wish I'd done things differently. I should have asked my father to escort me down the first half of the aisle and for John to take me the rest of the way to the altar to signify who had been around for each part of my life thus far. At the time I totally blamed my mother for keeping my father away, but today, older and wiser, I know better. There are no victims, only volunteers.

Today was my wedding day, so I told myself that I must be in love, and I wasn't going to allow anything to spoil it. This wedding gave me what I desperately needed, attention. The bride is the focus and the center of attention on her wedding day. I planned to relish the occasion. My need for attention was far greater than the quiet voice inside of me telling me, *This isn't right.*

After I changed into my wedding dress, I stood in front of the full-length mirror and marveled at the soon-to-be-married lady who smiled back at me in a full-length silk gown. The bodice of the gown was beaded with a V-neck, and the waistline was fitted with a straight skirt. I carried a bouquet of roses and lilies.

Over two hundred guests showed up for our wedding at the Calamigos Ranch in Malibu, and to my surprise my mother and John were among them. My handsome father beamed proudly as he walked me down the aisle, and I felt like a princess bride on his strong, steady arm. I was a little girl with her daddy, at last.

The sun was setting when Randy and I spoke our vows in the late spring. We each had written letters that we read during the ceremony. It was a touching and romantic ceremony, but as I look back now I see that what we thought was love was based on the fact that we enjoyed doing a lot of the same things together. We had common interests, but sadly, we lacked anything else.

The ceremony was beautiful, and when the minister pronounced us man and wife and then instructed Randy to kiss his bride, the guests applauded for Mr. and Mrs. Randy Brown.

I kissed my groom and then went to change into my dancing shoes and attire. As the country music blared on the stereo, I was busy changing into a fancy pair of white jeans so I could cut a rug at my wedding reception. I still wore my wedding veil as Randy twirled me around the dance floor. After the first dance with my new husband, my father led me by the hand across the floor and took me in his arms for the traditional father-daughter dance. It meant so much to me to have this moment. Unfortunately it was an intimacy I never shared with him. It felt more akward than how I had imagined it to be.

Afterward, I looked around the reception for John as my next dance partner, but he was nowhere to be found. My mother and John were so upset that I hadn't asked John to walk me down the aisle that they'd split right after the wedding ceremony. John missed out on an incredible father-daughter moment that might never come again. I felt cheated, but my sadness soon subsided when everyone joined us on the dance floor. As long as I was dancing, I felt happy.

Sadly, when the music ended, so did my joy. Reality hit. Now I had to face the real world of marriage, and I knew I was ill prepared. *Oh, well,* I comforted myself. *I can always get a divorce if this marriage doesn't work out.*

After the wedding Randy and I left in a shower of rice for our honeymoon trip to Hawaii. Throughout the honeymoon, I assumed the role of wife as an actress playing the part of the happy new bride. We stayed at the luxurious Ritz-Carlton for a week. Admittedly, I had fun with Randy, but in retrospect I was not in love with him. Something was missing.

As I sat on a beautiful beach and watched the sunset, I asked myself, *Is this all there is?* I felt so empty inside. I thought being married would fill that void. I thought it would give me security and the love I so desperately was seeking, but even though I believed Randy truly loved me, I had such a callused heart that I couldn't receive his love. I had grown so cynical. Every man in my life had disappointed me and I knew he would too.

Only Jesus will never disappoint you. While man's promises frequently are broken, Christ promises hold true. *Put no more trust in man, who has only breath in his nostrils. What is he really worth?* (Isa. 2:22).

Upon our return from our honeymoon, Randy and I moved in with his family in order to save money so we could eventually buy a home. I got along so well with him and his parents. As strange as it may seem it was more like Randy and I were brother and sister and marrying him is how I was adopted into this family. Yet, always waiting for the next tragedy to befall me, I still had that uneasy feeling on the inside that prevented me from enjoying my marriage as a new bride should. Something was just not right. I felt as though I was sitting on a time bomb that was about to explode.

Chapter 10

The Honeymoon
Is Over

I couldn't even boil potatoes over the heat of our affection.
Your love would never bridge a gap;
It wouldn't even fill up the hole that the mice came through.

—DJUNA BARNES

N ow that Randy and I were settled, and he'd gone back to work, I focused on my acting career.

Recently I'd followed my commercial agent from Irena's office to another agency, L.A. Talent, with hopes to land some representation with a theatrical agent so I could audition for roles in television and film as well as commercials. I had grown as an actress, and it was time for me to move up in the business.

As soon as I made the move, Joseph Berg, who handled L.A. Talent's theatrical clients, met with me and took an immediate liking to me. I sat in Joseph's office while he picked up the phone to

pitch me to a client. *Pitch* is another Hollywood term, which basically means to sell you to the casting directors, the directors, and
the producers, and sometimes, the studio executives. I found it sur-
real to hear someone say I was such a great actress and how much
potential I had, but those were words that slipped easily from
Joseph's lips. The prospect of getting into TV and film and Joseph's
confidence in my ability were encouraging to me. With an agent
like Joseph behind me, I felt like I could do anything.

Everything was falling beautifully into place for me at last. I felt
that someone truly believed in me. Just a day or so before my
wedding, Heinz Holba, the owner of the agency, had called me.
I assumed he was calling to welcome me into his fold, but when
told him I was getting married the next day, he asked me to call him
when I returned from my honeymoon.

Back in L.A., I picked up the phone to return Heinz's call.
I wondered what big audition he might have for me, so when he
answered the phone, I responded enthusiastically, "Hi Heinz,
I'm back from my honeymoon, and I'm raring to get to work."

There was a long pause at the other end of the line. Finally,
Heinz cleared his throat and said, "Tracy, I have some bad news
for you."

Uh-oh, I thought to myself. *Here it comes. Was he going to drop me
from his agency?* This is one of an actor's greatest fears because it's
nearly impossible to find another agent after losing one. Was he
dropping me from the agency because I'd gotten married? After
I became engaged, I was advised to keep my ring hidden during
auditions. Hollywood is about fantasy and I believed you had a better chance if the director and producer thought they might have a
chance with you.

"Tracy," Heinz hesitated, "Joseph Berg died."

"Died? What happened?" I was terribly upset over the news.

"Joseph killed himself," Heinz explained apologetically. "I didn't want to tell you. I knew the two of you were working well together, and I just couldn't spoil your wedding day with the news."

Poor Joseph Berg was another tragic Hollywood fatality. I wondered how many there were. The man escaped the emptiness of Hollywood by swallowing a bullet to end it all. He lived in a house in Beverly Hills and drove a big BMW, but come to find out, the house was empty, and he was broke. Joseph was playing the role, but it was all a facade. If I had only known Jesus at the time, I could have shared him with this desperate man.

I deeply mourned the passing of my biggest champion. Joseph was the first guy who believed in my talent as a film and television actress. The dark side of the entertainment business had claimed yet another victim. Trembling, I vowed this would never happen to me. *Therefore, whoever thinks he stands must be careful not to fall!* (*1 Cor. 10:12*).

Coming home from my honeymoon to the news of Joseph's death felt as though a door had been slammed in my face. Where would I go from here? So many times I felt as though I was playing Monopoly and picked the *Go to jail* card every time it was my turn.

Heinz soon introduced me to Carol, another agent, who was eventually successful in getting me several auditions. Exactly one month after I returned from my honeymoon, I got my first theatrical job, an NBC movie of the week, *Search and Rescue*, starring actor Robert Conrad.

Carol informed me that I would be on location in Bear, California, a remote community in northern California for four weeks. I was so excited I took the job immediately. After the wedding I suffered the usual wedding bell blues, but I was alarmed to realize that in many ways the separation from Randy was a welcome retreat. Was I emotionally incapable of being a wife? For me to play the role of the wife I believed was what is referred to in the movie industry as *bad casting*.

Randy was a great guy, but it was all about me. I was addicted to falling in love, but once I had captured my prey, I was eager for the next pursuit. I wanted to leave instead of being left and cheat instead of being cheated on.

Only a month ago I'd been on my honeymoon, and suddenly I was off on another adventure. When I arrived in northern California, the location manager led me to my living quarters, a darling little cottage nestled in the woods. I was delighted. It was summertime and everything was green and flowers were in bloom all around the cottage. Inside there was an open living area with a kitchen. My bedroom was upstairs in a loft.

The residents of Bear welcomed our cast and crew with open arms and our money with outstretched hands. Within a few days we had taken over the town, which consisted of one restaurant and a gas station. The cast and crew did a lot of socializing and quickly developed a deep camaraderie.

Two cute twin brothers my age, Kent and Karl Bennett, immediately became my constant companions. Only back from my honeymoon a month, and already my eyes were wandering. After a few days, I picked out the twin who most appealed to me.

Flirting shamelessly with Kent, I recognized in him the same spirit of lust that was in me. I didn't fight the attraction either. On the set one day I intentionally complained of how creepy my cabin was and confessed that I was so afraid that I had a difficult time sleeping. How cleverly I perfected the role of the damsel in distress to lure the prey into my web. Gentlemanly Kent immediately volunteered to sleep on the sofa in my living room in order to keep me company. What a splendid idea!

Kent didn't stay on that sofa for more than a few hours that first night until I had enticed him into my bedroom. Sadly, a month after I married, I cheated on my husband, and I continued to cheat on him with Kent for the duration of the filming. *Do not commit adultery (Exod. 20:14)*. I'd broken this commandment again, this time in my mind to a greater extent since I'd betrayed my husband. This time the sin didn't just involve two willing people but also an innocent victim. Since I was a married woman, I'd broken the commandment in the true sense of the word.

After two weeks at the film location, I was surprised to get a call from Randy to say that he was driving up to visit me for my birthday the next weekend. This unexpected news sent me into a complete tailspin. I knew I ran the risk of being caught. I couldn't imagine having Randy and Kent around at the same time.

I had to kick Kent out of my bed to make room for my husband. Although he was my husband, he felt like the outsider in the crowd when he arrived. Thanks to my acting skills, I survived the weekend, but as soon as Randy left, I hopped right back into bed with Kent. He acted hurt and said he felt betrayed by my husband's appearance. You know you have it backward when your boyfriend complains when you spend time with your husband. To comfort him I spent the remainder of the nights during the film shoot with Kent.

My affair with Kent Bennett ended with the job, and I returned to L.A. to my husband's bed as if nothing had happened. I assumed my role as an actor, so I was able to adjust to the marriage. Tragically, this scenario is common on location shoots. It's so commonplace that often no one even raises an eyebrow.

Before long Randy and I decided that we needed to be out on our own. Part of it was my guilt in facing his parents day after day after what I'd done. They'd not only paid for our wedding, but they'd been so good to me. They treated me like a daughter, and this was how I thanked them. If they only knew what I'd done to their son, I was sure they would kick me out of their house. Even though they had no idea, I felt that I was walking around like Hester Prynne from the pages of the book *The Scarlet Letter* by Nathaniel Hawthorne, with a scarlet *A* stamped on my forehead. I was relieved when we finally moved out of their house.

I thought moving would absolve my guilt, but even when you move, your problems go with you. To my surprise one night we were watching TV, and Randy asked out of the blue, "Was anything going on between you and that Kent Bennett?"

I was dumbfounded. Naturally, I denied it and even went so far as to act insulted.

"I know something happened," Randy pressed on.

"Well, it didn't."

"I don't believe you."

"How dare you not believe me? Are you calling me a liar?" He continued to insist that things didn't seem right. He had such good instincts.

Seeing my tactics weren't working, I quickly switched them and only revealed enough of the truth to satisfy his accusations without getting myself into hot water. "You're right. He tried to kiss me." This is where my acting skills really came in handy. Like any good soap actor, I laid it on so thick I easily could have won a Daytime Emmy with my performance of denial.

"It was just awful, but I didn't tell you because I didn't want to hurt you. But I swear it was only a kiss. Nothing else happened."

It's so easy to convince someone who doesn't really want to know the truth, so a look of pity appeared in Randy's eyes. Instead of berating me anymore, he ended up comforting poor little old me.

I was relieved I had fooled him.

I knew I had tainted our relationship, and I hoped that moving into our own place, a cute one-bedroom townhouse in Woodland Hills would give us a fresh start. It wasn't easy for me to be pure of heart, but I was making my best efforts. I justified my behavior as sinners always do. "I'm young. What he doesn't know won't hurt him." I had become a master at living a parallel life. Hurting people who cared about me was exactly what my mother and grandmother had conditioned me to do.

On the night of January 16, 1994, we hosted a lovely dinner party for friends in our new townhouse. It had been a wonderful evening, and I was feeling domestic and romantic. I felt like a real wife. For the first time in a long time I slept peacefully. At approximately 4:20 a.m. the next morning, an explosion rudely awakened Randy and me. Crash! Boom! Bang!

As the earth creaked and groaned, I thought, *It's the end of the world.* Over and over again, I kept murmuring, "Oh my God. Oh my God." It was as though good and evil had both risen up out of the earth, and the battle had begun.

Like a knight in shining armor, Randy jumped into action. He grabbed me and pushed me to the end of the bed and jumped on top of me to protect me from falling objects. It was not a second too soon, for the motorcycle helmets above our bed and the mirrored headboard came crashing down on the spot where we had lain. Glass flew and sliced Randy's back and arms. Underneath him I was still screaming, "Oh my God! Oh my God!" Even though I was not a Christian, I was calling on God to save me. *Therefore we will not be afraid, though the earth trembles and the mountains topple into the depths of the seas, though its waters roar and foam and the mountains quake with its turmoil (Ps. 46:2–3).*

Awful sounds were coming from everywhere; the doors were slamming, the glass was breaking, and the brick was falling off the fireplace. Everything in the kitchen cabinets was falling and breaking.

"It's the end of the world," I whimpered again. I felt physically ill, but my husband comforted me as he nuzzled me in his arms.

In approximately fifteen seconds, the Northridge Earthquake was all over, but it was fifteen seconds of pure hell and what seemed like an eternity. Randy got me to listen long enough to tell me that we had to go check on his folks and my sisters. I agreed and gladly got out of the house. It felt like it was haunted inside, and I was terrified it would cave in on us at any second.

We had no electricity, no phone, and no gas. Near the epicenter of the quake with a magnitude of 6.8 on the Richter scale, our home was badly hit. An eerie darkness fell all around us, and when we tried to get to our car to get away, we couldn't get the garage door open. We walked outside, but the guard gates that surrounded our apartment wouldn't open either. We were trapped.

Randy physically lifted the garage door enough so I could slide under and release the door manually. I was terrified to go in for fear of another aftershock. Randy had everything under control so I trusted him. Driving over to his parents' home, we witnessed destruction everywhere. It was a terrifying sight. Our city looked like a bombed-out war zone. This 6.8 earthquake was reported to have caused over $44 billion in damage and was deemed the most disastrous quake in US history. Because of the early hour of the quake, 4:30 a.m., there were fewer than seventy-five deaths. No one could deny that the timing of this earthquake was truly God's protection.

Once again we moved in with Randy's family. Our building looked as though it would fall down at any minute. The chimney had fallen, and the stairs had separated. We stayed there longer than necessary because I was so terrified that I refused to return to our apartment even after it was repaired.

Unable to calm myself, I learned I was suffering from an acute case of post-traumatic stress. I couldn't go alone into our townhouse or anywhere else. Every day I'd go to work with Randy at the crack of dawn and sleep in the back office until the sun came up, and then I'd drive to a friend's house to get dressed for auditions or work. This was another example of what a devoted husband Randy was. A lot of men would have been too proud to let their cowardly wife come to work with them in her pajamas and sleep in the shop. But Randy loved me, and his loyalties were always to me first. At the time I couldn't recognize this quality.

Unfortunately, I had yet to learn that "safety does not exist in the absence of danger, but in the presence of God."[3] As the Book of Psalm says, *Even when I go through the darkest valley, I fear no danger, for You are with me; Your rod and Your staff—they comfort me (23:4)*.

Eventually things calmed down, and our lives went back to normal, but something magical had happened in our marriage during this time. Having survived the tragedy together, Randy and I bonded in a deeper, more meaningful way.

Chapter 11

Trouble in Paradise

Of this you can be sure, my dearest,
Whatever thy life befall,
The cross that our own hands fashion is the heaviest cross of all.
—KATHERINE ELEANOR CONWAY, "THE HEAVIEST CROSS OF ALL"

After we settled down from the trauma of the earthquake, Randy and I slowly began to enjoy life again. As a result, I developed more self-confidence, and my outlook on life became more positive. I began to delight in spending time with my husband.

A great escape that Randy and I enjoyed together was riding his "iron horse," a motorcycle. Randy would rev it up, I'd jump on the back, and we'd speed away down the highway. In many ways I related this freedom on the open road to riding my horse. I loved holding onto my husband as he turned the curves throughout the beautiful state of California down the coast, into the canyons, and up to the mountains.

One beautiful, sunny California day we were driving down a boulevard when a car ran a stop sign and pulled out in front of us. Smack! We almost escaped the accident, but our bike clipped their trunk and Randy's elbow went through the rear window of the car. I flew headfirst over the trunk. I knew I was hurt, but I was afraid to look down at my body to see how badly.

Again, my husband donned his imaginary cape and became my superhero. Neither he nor I had any idea what was wrong with me, but I was in pain. Randy sat Indian style with my head in his lap and comforted me. Once we arrived at the hospital, the doctor discovered I had a deep two-inch tear. Because I had squeezed my legs together so tightly, when we hit the other car, the impact jerked my legs apart and split me in two.

Because the other car was at fault, we were awarded some money for the injuries, which we later found included my neck, my back, and my jaw. No longer did we have to wait to buy a house. We wisely used the insurance money for our downpayment.

Years ago, I had met a girl in my aerobics class who'd bought a home before she hit twenty-five, and that became my goal too. I reached my goal; we bought our home just before my twenty-fifth birthday. We turned our unfortunate circumstances into a winning endeavor. Our lives improved with each passing day.

Randy and I purchased a house in Tarzana in the San Fernando Valley. I was officially a Valley girl, a term used throughout the nation that basically meant I was cool!

Randy and I loved working together on the house to get it into shape. We even strung lights so we were able to work well into the night. Since Randy was a carpenter, we were able to do amazing things to the house and the yard. Together we transformed our home into a little showplace. I realize now that Randy and I stayed busy all the time. In an effort to avoid emotional intimacy, we stayed busy. Randy and I were human *doers*, not human *beings*.

Just as we were getting settled into our newly renovated home, I was cast for a role in a TV show that was filmed overseas. This was the first overseas job I'd booked and my first trip outside the country. I asked Randy to accompany me, but he was unable to get off work for two weeks.

Next I called my grandmother and begged her to go with me. With my per diem, the daily stipend given for food and necessities while on location, I could pay all of my grandmother's expenses. In spite of my pleas, she didn't feel up to going out of the country, so I was forced to go alone. From the deep wounds of my childhood, I had developed a profound fear of being alone, so this was part of the reason I felt desperate to have someone accompany me.

As soon I stepped off the plane, I went straight to the hotel. When actors travel overseas, the union requires its actors to fly first-class and to be put up in five-star hotels. The hotel was beautiful. After I'd settled into my luxurious room, the phone rang. To my surprise it was the star of the show calling to welcome me.

The star of the show was friendly and asked if I needed anything. Being an American, he said he understood that it was sometimes difficult to travel to a foreign country to work. His inquiry appeared to me to be a normal courtesy call.

Later I learned that he had seen my head shot when one of the producers had flashed it and said, "Wait till you see the actress we have coming for the next episode." Once again I misrepresented myself. I had hidden my weddding ring on the audition. I never took my husbands last name professtionally either.

I innocently asked the actor if he knew anyplace nearby where I could work out. "Why don't you work out with me?" he gallantly offered. I said yes, and he was more than happy to oblige and even offered to pick me up and take me there.

I was doomed when I accepted. I was kidding myself that it was only a workout. Of course something between the two of us developed over the short time I was there. Ever the romantic, I fell madly in love with this handsome hunk, and we were together constantly the two weeks I was out of the country.

When the show ended, I didn't want to leave. I had already made up my mind that if this actor asked me to stay with him, I would leave my husband and relocate to this foreign country immediately. He didn't ask me though. The combination of leaving and the angst I felt over not knowing how this famous actor really felt about me was just unbearable to me. On my flight back to L.A., I was blue, heartbroken. I was like a junkie who needed her next love fix to be happy.

I called the actor a few times, but he had a girlfriend with him overseas now, and along with the time difference, it made it impossible for us to connect. A few weeks later the phone rang, and it was the actor. When I hung up the phone, I was walking on clouds. He told me that he was in town doing a publicity stunt on the *Tonight Show*. "Can you sneak over to the hotel for a little while?"

The knowledge that a famous actor wanted to sleep with me made me feel special. I was over there and in bed with the actor in a flash! Every time he came to California, my phone would ring. I'd give Randy some flimsy excuse, sneak over to the actor's hotel, and crawl into bed with him. After this happened several times, it finally occurred to me that I was nothing but a sex object to him. He never took me out to dinner, and he refused to be seen in public. I was outraged. Celebrity adulterers have to be more careful than the average Joe. They can be caught more easily because they are more recognized.

Every time I complained about our relationship, he'd remind me that I was the one who was married. But I wanted more of him.

I wanted to go places with him and get the celebrity treatment being on his important arm. Truthfully, I would have left my husband in a minute for the television star but he never asked me. I saw the writing on the wall. I was easy and safe for this man. Every time I made love with him, I realized that sleeping with a celebrity didn't give me self-worth at all; it made me feel worthless.

Rejected, I went back to my husband, more determined to try to make the best of it. It took me a while to get over the television star, but I soon became content in marriage.

In January, Randy told me he was going skiing with a friend, David Wallace, and begged me to come along. I suggested that they have a ski trip just for the guys since it was pilot season and an actor always stays close by the phone from January through May because most new shows are cast during this period. Randy never liked being away from me, but since he was only going away for the day, he agreed.

I kissed Randy good-bye, and he and his friend drove up to Snow Summit for the day. Randy was an extreme sports person. He was into fast motorcycles and was also a great snow skier. He was really looking forward to a day on the slopes. That's the wonderful thing about living in L.A.; within two hours you can be snow skiing in the mountains or sunning on the beach.

I was spending a quiet Saturday at home when my phone rang around five o'clock in the afternoon. It was Pam, a close friend of ours. "What up?" I asked her.

"There's been an accident, Tracy."

She didn't have to say another word. I knew it was Randy.

"David called and asked me to call you," Pam explained. "He's with Randy."

"Is he OK?"

"Tracy, Randy has been badly injured in a ski accident, and he's been airlifted to a trauma center."

The news rendered me speechless. Pam explained that another friend of ours, Jeff, was on his way now to pick me up to take me to Randy's side. My husband's friends felt obligated to protect me and take care of me. It was at least a ninety-mile trek. Jeff drove me up there weaving in and out of traffic, but it seemed to take us forever to get there. Deep in thought over Randy, both of us were unusually quiet. What Jeff hadn't told me was that they weren't sure if Randy would survive.

Once we arrived at the hospital, David rushed up to greet us. He hugged me and explained the details of the accident. David was skiing down the mountain to watch Randy make a big jump, but when he turned around, he saw Randy sliding down the mountain on his face. When he reached him, he was unconscious. The ski patrol arrived, and they took Randy by ambulance to the hospital. David handed me Randy's necklace. Seeing the broken gold chain upset me because this was a special necklace that he never took off. I clasped it in my hand and held it close to my heart.

After I had anxiously waited for what seemed like an eternity, the nurse came into the waiting room and told me she would take me back.

"May my friends go in there with me?" I asked her. Without the support of our friends, I wasn't sure I could handle seeing Randy in his condition.

"I'm sorry, only one person at a time is allowed in there, but don't worry, I'll be with you." The nurse replied as she took my hand and squeezed it and led me down the endless corridor.

Just before we walked through the door to intensive care, the nurse suddenly stopped and looked me straight in the eyes. "Tracy, I need to prepare you for what you're about to see. When Randy fell, he slid face first down the mountain. He has freezer burn down one side of his face and is covered in bruises. His lower lip is unattached and it's hanging off to one side. We've induced a coma so we could run some tests. He's unconscious, but his eyes are open."

I took a deep breath.

"Are you ready to see him now?"

I nodded; assuring the nurse I would be fine, I followed her through the door. Nothing could have prepared me for the way he looked. Everything the nurse had described was true, only multiplied by a factor of ten. Randy was unconscious and his eyes were the most horrifying sight. Wide open, they were bulging out of his head. Seeing my husband in that condition was the hardest thing I ever witnessed.

Anxiously I kept a vigil at Randy's beside. Days passed and then a week. Back in L.A., it was pilot season, so I had to call my agent to book out indefinitely. I explained to my agent that I was needed at my husband's side.

"Are you a doctor?" my agent snapped unsympathetically.

"No, but when he wakes up, I'd like to be here," I explained. My agent was not too happy, and normally an actor will do anything to please her agent. Without him, she is nothing, but I didn't care if I ever worked again. If Randy recovered, I promised myself I would be a wonderful wife to him. I begged God to make my husband well. Although I didn't know the Lord, I was desperate and thought I could negotiate with him and get exactly what I wanted.

In the past I'd taken my husband for granted, but now that I was close to losing him, I'd sworn to myself that I'd never cheat on him again. The thought of losing him was devastating to me. As I sat there night after night, I began to worry what would happen to my marriage if Randy found out I had cheated on him. If he did, I knew that I would lose him, and I no longer wanted to let him go. Why did I sabotage a good thing?

After a week my husband finally opened his eyes. My first thought was, *Wow! God really did answer my prayers.* Yet when Randy spoke, his mother, who had kept the vigil with me, and I were shocked. This California born and bred strapping guy now spoke in a deep Southern accent.

"What is causing that?" I asked the doctor.

The doctor shrugged. "Even doctors don't fully understand the complexities of the brain, but what I do know is that the fall was so hard it shoved his brain to the back of his head, causing damage on the front and the rear parts of the brain." The doctor explained that Randy had damaged the area of his brain that controls his rationale and reasoning.

From this description I reasoned that Randy's eggs had gotten scrambled and I was determined that I was going to be the faithful wife and nurse who would help him unscramble them. I looked at the doctor and asked, "How long will it take for him to heal?"

The doctor shrugged. "He'll keep getting better until he stops getting better. There's no way to predict the extent of the damage with a head injury. Nor can we predict how your husband might behave. He will likely have the mental capacity of a five-year-old boy and the physical capacity of a man.

"If I were you, I wouldn't stay at home alone with him," the doctor recommended. "With the rationale and reasoning part of his brain damaged, he will emulate a drunk person, and just as drunk people often take on different personalities, so will he. So we can't predict if he will become amorous or violent. Do you have family the two of you could stay with until Randy improves?"

Of course my in-laws welcomed us back into their home. Just as the doctor predicted, Randy's behavior was bizarre. He'd look at me and say in his newly acquired Southern accent, "Get me some supper, woman."

Forcing a smile, I tried to do whatever he asked until his sexual demands were unbearable. Morning, noon, and night, Randy was like a teenager who had discovered sex for the first time. He spoke to me disrespectfully, and I didn't know how to handle his crude comments. His parents were supportive and helpful to me throughout this dreadful ordeal.

Months went by and Randy progressed slowly. His mom looked into all kinds of ways to help her son, and she finally found a doctor to monitor his brain activity. The doctor told us that emotionally Randy had flatlined, and as a result he had a nonemotional personality. Although Randy eventually did improve, he was somewhat of a stranger to me.

After several months his mother and I both decided that Randy had made enough progress for me to take him home. We believed that if he went back to his familiar routine he might improve.

Chapter 12

Dangerous Obsessions

Insanity is doing the same thing over and over again,
but expecting different results.

—Rita Mae Brown, *Sudden Death*

Back at home I soon discovered that there was nothing familiar about our routine. During this time I often felt like my husband had died that fateful day on the snowy mountain. Unable to work, Randy was at home all day long. Quickly bored, he started wanting to go out with his friends during the day. Besides being worried about him when he was away, it also disturbed me greatly that he wanted to go out with his friends. In the past Randy had wanted to spend all his time with me. He never even went out with the guys. That all changed.

During the day his friends would stop by the house and pick him up and take him to the beach. While I was out on auditions, Randy was at the beach playing volleyball or rollerblading with his buddies. I became concerned when I noticed a girl who was hanging out with them and was always flirting with Randy and he, with her. When I told him it bothered me, he was enraged. He accused me of acting like his mother and said that I just didn't want him to have any fun. After this I noticed that he began to pull away from me.

Strangely, our roles suddenly reversed. I was the devoted, stay-at-home wife, and he became the wandering husband. In his eyes I became holier than thou, obsessively possessive, and insanely jealous. I had to admit that his perception was true. When he was out night or day, I imagined all sorts of things had happened to him. Having almost lost Randy, I appreciated my husband so much more than I had previously. I was clinging to him for dear life. I was suffering the consequences of my own actions. Was I being punished for being unfaithful to my husband? This doubt made me all the more insecure, and the more insecure I felt, the more I nagged him.

It's no surprise that Randy rebelled, and the fighting between us began. In his book *Love Must Be Tough*, Dr. James C. Dobson explains, "Nothing destroys a romantic relationship more quickly than for a person to throw himself, weeping and clinging, on the back of the cool partner to beg for mercy. That infuses the wayward spouse with an even greater desire to escape from the leech that threatens to suck his life's blood. He may pity the wounded partner and wish that things were different, but he can rarely bring himself to love again under those circumstances."[4]

Prior to Randy's accident, we'd only had minor disagreements, but now we were having knockdown drag outs and screaming matches. One night when he hadn't come home, I decided to wait up for him to confront him. Because of his illness, I'd tried to tread lightly in the past, but tonight I'd reached my limit; I'd had enough. When he finally showed up in the middle of the night, I was waiting at the door for him, full of rage.

"Where've you been?" I demanded to know.

"Out."

"Have you been drinking?" I sounded more accusatory than questioning.

"A few margaritas," he confessed.

I reminded him that this was a definite no-no according to his doctor.

"I'm not talking about this. I'm going to bed." Randy replied emphatically.

I wouldn't let up on him and followed him into our bedroom. As he got ready for bed, I kept demanding to know where he'd been and what he'd done.

Again he told me he wasn't going to discuss it, that he was going to bed. He jumped into bed and under the covers.

"If you love me, you'll talk to me," I pleaded. I should have backed off, but I was so consumed with anger that I was out of control. Determined that Randy wasn't going to treat me this way, I made unreasonable demands on him. I was like a two-year-old who didn't get her way and then threw a temper tantrum. Hadn't I earned that privilege? I'd faithfully stood by Randy throughout his accident and his recovery; he owed me. I was determined that he was going to give me the respect I deserved or else. I would not tolerate being ignored. This time when he rejected my attempts to talk to him again, I picked up the mattress and literally threw him out of bed.

"Our marriage is at stake," I told him. "We have to talk about this now."

Thinking he would give in if I threatened him, I said, "Fine, you have two choices: Tomorrow I'll call a marriage counselor or a divorce attorney."

"Go ahead and call the attorney," he said without any emotion.

Without a word I flew into a rage. I grabbed a suitcase out of the closet and flung it open and began packing my clothes. I was making so much noise, but it didn't seem to faze him. Why isn't he stopping me? The more he didn't react, the more I turned up the drama. I screamed; then I'd pack some more. His rejection was more than I could bear. What was worse, he didn't react to me at all.

Much to my disappointment, Randy didn't appear to care, so I stalked out of the bedroom and into the living room. For a while I paced around the room roaring like an angry lioness in search of her prey, wondering what to attack next. Spotting photographs of our smiling faces encased in ornate frames on a nearby table, I stared at them. Then I picked them up one by one and started hurling the frames against the wall. The frames crashed, and the glass shattered upon the floor.

Suddenly I felt the intensity of a tornado coming down the hallway. His outrage was so frightening that I ran out of the house and jumped into my car. He followed me and put his hand inside the car door just as I was about to close it. He opened the car door with such force that it was dented by the muffler of his motorcycle parked next to it.

I realized I'd gone too far. All I had wanted was for him to care about me and stop me from leaving. He stopped me all right. Reaching inside, Randy clasped his hands around my throat, then he yanked me out of the car by the neck and threatened to break my neck.

"Get back in the house right now," he warned, his eyes flashing with anger. Something rose up inside of me, but suddenly for the first time in my life, I found my voice. I began to yell so loudly that my voice frightened even me as my screams echoed throughout the neighborhood. He dragged me into the house.

Inside the house he threw me on the sofa and jumped on top of me. He began yelling obscenities that I'm obliged to omit, "I loved you, but you treated me like dirt!" he yelled. You deceived me. I never believed your lies. I know you cheated on me with Kent. I thought you were this nice country girl, but you fooled me; you're nothing but an uppity phony Hollywood witch."

"No," I screamed. "Please Randy, please, I love you."

Ignoring me, he continued yelling, "I could kill you right now for what you've done to me."

I knew with all my heart that Randy was serious. A wild look appeared in his eyes that I'd never seen in a person before or since. Filled with such rage and hatred, Randy threatened me again, as he lifted a hand to me. Truly fearing for my life, I begged him for mercy, but he wouldn't respond. "Please believe me, I do love you, Randy." I pleaded with the little strength I had left inside of me. I apologized for hurting him. I promised to change.

Ignoring me, Randy reached for my throat and squeezed my neck with his bare hands. A cynical smile curled at his lips. "Do you know how easily I could kill you right now?" He repeated these same words over and over again.

This is it, I thought to myself. I squeezed my eyes shut, when suddenly a bright light from outside shone through the windows and lit up the room.

Quickly loosening his fingers around my neck, Randy called out, "Who is it?"

Fortunately for me, Randy's anger was transferred to the person who was shining the light upon our darkness.

"Open up. It's the police," a deep voice called out. Then the man pounded on the door.

Not wanting the cops to come inside to witness the scene, Randy jumped up at once and opened the door. Despite the fact that Randy was still in his underwear, he went outside. I could hear the voices of the policemen.

The cop said, "A neighbor said they heard screams coming from your house and called us. Do you want to tell us what's going on?"

After all these years someone had finally heard my cry for help in the darkness. For the first time in my life, I had finally called out for help, and I got it! All along I didn't know the meaning of Jesus' words, seek and you will find, ask and receive. *"Keep asking, and it will be given to you. Keep searching, and you will find. Keep knocking, and the door will be opened to you. For everyone who asks receives, and the one who searches finds, and to the one who knocks, the door will be opened" (Matt. 7:7–8).*

No one was more surprised than I that someone had come to my rescue. I sat there in a daze, knowing that someone up there cared about me. If the neighbors hadn't called and the police hadn't come, I'm fully convinced that Randy would have killed me. He had crossed that line between reason and rationale and had totally lost control.

"Where's your wife?" one of the cops asked.

I straightened my clothes and went out on the porch to assure them I was OK, but one of the cops took me aside. They separated us and began to interrogate us. As a result of Nicole Simpson's brutal murder, L.A. cops had become attentive to domestic abuse, and they made clear that they weren't leaving until they were sure we were both OK.

"Has your husband ever hurt you before?" one of the policemen asked me.

"No, he's never laid a hand on me. This is the first time. We just had an argument."

Next thing I know the cop leans over to examine my neck.

"Are those your husband's handprints around your neck?" My neck had deep red finger marks and he also noticed that my lip was bleeding.

"Sorry, lady," the policeman apologized. "We're taking your husband to jail."

"Please don't do that," I pleaded. "This was all my fault. I antagonized him."

"That's no reason for him to try to strangle you."

The cop explained it was no longer required for a victim to press charges. If there were any visible marks they were required to arrest. After Nicole Simpson's murder, the L.A. cops weren't taking any chances. Even though I had provoked Randy, there was nothing I could say or do to keep them from hauling Randy away to jail.

Nothing I could say to the police would change their minds. I watched silently as they loaded Randy into the police car. He was livid, and it was obvious that he blamed me. Another obstacle for us. Although no one deserves to be beaten, the reality was that I had played an equal part in this mess.

Upset, I went back into the house and phoned his mom right away. I was surprised by her response, which I realize now was a normal one. She was totally unsympathetic toward him. "Randy can stay in jail tonight as far as I'm concerned," she insisted.

I was still shaking. I did not want to be alone, so I called my good friend Chris Chauncey, who was in my acting class, and she came over to spend the night with me.

Also due to the Nicole Simpson incident, I found out the next morning that a restraining order against an abuser was automatically put into effect the next day. Fearing Randy's wrath, I tried to get the order lifted and the charges dropped, but the police don't take lightly to the abuse victim wanting to drop these charges. Since we had no history of domestic violence and Randy had no record, I felt hopeful that I could straighten this mess out because all I wanted was to fix things and get my husband back home.

This process was frustrating. I tried to get the charges against Randy dropped. They immediately connected me with a victim's advocate. The advocate totally refused to believe it was the first time this had ever happened. They are trained to understand the mind of an abused woman. They kept repeating in a condescending voice, "I know you're frightened, and it's embarrassing. If you don't try to get him off, he'll be even angrier at you when he's released." To them, my words sounded like those of an abused woman defending her abuser.

Randy's mom was still totally disgusted over the incident. She didn't defend what her son had done. Instead, she was supportive of me. Had she known the kind of wife I'd been to him behind closed doors, I doubt she would have had so much sympathy for me.

Randy eventually was released, and after a lot of effort I was able to get the restraining order removed. The court sentenced him to fifty hours of community service and ordered him to complete an anger management course, but his anger for me remained. He clearly thought this incident was my fault, and I knew deep down inside that a part of it was. Randy had nothing but contempt for me. He had a felony on his record, and he blamed me for it. I forgave him and begged him to forgive me and to come back home.

Agreeing to move back in with me, Randy took a separate room and spent most of his time on the phone, ignoring me. This time he didn't just go out during the day while I was working, but he began to frequent the country bars alone at night. You can't cheat a cheater no matter how hard you try. When he left the house, I would pick up the phone and hit redial. To my disgust I reached a topless bar, the Candy Cat.

Later I also discovered that Randy was talking to a girl he'd met through his community service for domestic violence. I warned this woman to stay away from my husband, but sadly, I knew if she disappeared, Randy would just find someone else. He was through with me.

Resently, Randy had returned to work. Most nights Randy would come home from work and shower, then he would slather himself with cologne and go out dancing at a country bar. This was painful to me because I knew how popular he was at the country bars. Wooed by Randy myself, I knew the power he had on the dance floor in his cowboy hat and smooth moves.

I desperately wanted to turn my marriage around, and I naively believed that it would improve. I told myself that Randy was sick, and soon he'd get well, but with each passing day our marriage only grew worse.

On my wedding day I looked into Randy's eyes and spoke the vow, "in sickness and in health," without fully comprehending the reality of the words. Recently, the circumstances of my husband's accident had brough me to a place of understanding the vow and I seriously took it to heart. In the past every time our marriage survived a trauma, it was as though by some supernatural strength we overcame these adversities and bonded on an even deeper level. Because Randy and I had survived these challenges, there was no way I was going to give up and walk away from my vows now. No matter how difficult our marriage became, I was determined to honor my vows even the one I broke the most, forsaking all others.

Randy had somehow gotten a black box from a friend that enabled him to get all the cable channels. Whenever I would walk into the living room, he was always watching porn channels. It was incredibly shameful for me because he would barely glance up at me when I'd come in the room and try to talk to him. He would go back to watching the filth on the screen and ignore me.

Desperate to find answers, I discovered that Randy kept his large toolbox locked in the garage. Unsuccessful in picking the lock, I phoned a locksmith to open the toolbox for me when Randy was out dancing one night. Just as I suspected, I discovered a stash of pornographic magazines and movies inside, but when I dug even deeper, what I hadn't expected to find were divorce papers.

There they were, hidden away, but it was obvious that Randy had a plan to serve me with these papers. Randy hadn't served the papers on me yet, but they were pending.

Ranting and raving, I paced the floor, waiting for him to come home so I could confront him. The minute he walked in the door, all hell broke loose. Again I lost it and totally freaked out. Fortunately for me, because Randy was on probation after having beaten me before, he couldn't lay a hand on me or else he would go to jail. To his credit, he was taking anger management courses, and he had learned how to handle his temper. Having learned his lesson, he refused to lay a hand on me because he never wanted to go back to jail again.

Of course when Randy ignored me, I became even more hysterical. I finally realized that no matter what I did, I wasn't going to get a reaction from him unless I used desperate means, so I ran into the bathroom and threatened to kill myself. I believed that this foolish attempt would let him know just how much I loved him. I tried to use this suicide attempt to control my circumstances. I was pathetic. I thought I could use my suffering to gain his sympathy and regain his love.

Randy just stood there and watched me gobble codeine pills down my throat and chase them with beer. Turning around, I fell to my knees and begged Randy not to leave me. His face was vacant, except for a shred of disgust. I had never felt sicker in my entire life. I ran out of the house and jumped into my car.

Randy had refused to touch me—even to save my life—for fear of going back to jail. He wisely called my friend Heather to come to my aid.

Heather got me on my cell phone before I even got out of the neighborhood and convinced me to go back home. She would meet me there. When Heather walked in the door, I could tell by the look on her face that she was horrified to see me. I was sitting on the sofa chain-smoking cigarettes and watching one of Randy's porn flicks. If you can't beat 'em, join 'em. As she moved closer, she gagged from the stench of the tequila and beer in which I'd been drowning myself before she got there.

Not surprising, I don't remember much about this night; other than suffering worked again. Heather managed to get Randy to sleep next to me that night to make sure I didn't choke on my vomit. He also agreed to go to counseling with me.

After everything that happened, I knew Heather was right. I desperately needed help, and I had needed it for a long time. I'd just been afraid to ask for it. Now I was desperate to keep my husband from abandoning me, so I was willing to try anything. Since I hadn't been successful at winning him back, maybe a psychiatrist could tell me how.

A few days later I flipped through the names listed on my Screen Actor's Guild Insurance in search of a psychiatrist. Dr. Doctor. I looked at the print more closely. Surely, this was a misprint, but out of curiosity, I dialed the telephone number. It was no misprint. My method of choosing a counselor was bizarre, but again God must have been looking out for me. Dr. Doctor was a marriage counselor who specialized in sexual addiction? This choice proved to be a divine appointment. I liked Dr. Doctor instantly.

I begged Randy to accompany me to the counselor, and he finally agreed to go. The doctor patiently listened to our tale of woe and then told us, "You can't go on living like this. The two of you have to decide what to do about your marriage."

Truthfully, Randy wanted to save our marriage, but he couldn't get past all the hurt and pain I caused him by having the affair with Kent. He was already seeking comfort from other women, a common trait of a man whose wife has betrayed him.

I was distraught all the time over Randy, and my family and my friends grew concerned about me. My sister Kristine and I decided to get away for a few days, so we rented a little cabin and decided to go skiing. Of course, nothing helped me in the state I was in, and I insisted on coming home earlier than we planned.

As I drove up to my house, I spotted Randy's car in the driveway. My heart leaped. I was ecstatic that he was home until I also saw a strange car parked outside the house on the street. "Aha! I've caught him." This infuriated me. In a rage I jumped out of the car.

The house was dark with only a flicker coming from the TV screen in the living room. When I flipped on the lights and saw my husband cuddled on the sofa with a mutual friend of ours, Ann, along with her two-year-old daughter, I couldn't breathe.

"Well, just look at the cozy little family." I quipped.

They were surprised to see me, but neither of them reacted. This made me even more hysterical. With no regard for the young child, I started screaming for Ann to get out. Obscenities were spewing from my mouth. I'd done it again, broken another commandment. *Do not misuse the name of the LORD your God, because the LORD will punish anyone who misuses His name (Exod. 20:7).*

To my dismay, Randy immediately jumped to Ann's defense. Looking back, I am mortified that I behaved so badly with no regard for the toddler, but I had no impulse control back then.

Ann took her daughter in her arms and started to leave.

"Wait," Randy called to her. For a moment they stood staring at each other. Randy gave her a reassuring look. "Go on home. I'll be there in a moment."

This touching scene filled with Randy's concern for Ann and her daughter broke my heart. I had to witness my husband's loyalties to another woman instead of to me, his wife, in our home.

Although I had had affairs in the past, it was excruciating to have one rubbed in my face. Knowing I deserved it hurt all the more. I figured it was me who had put myself in this situation. I had gotten exactly what I deserved.

For the first time I realized that I had totally lost him. I sprawled out on the floor in my living room. Lying there in the darkness, all the depth of the sorrow and the loneliness in my life began to rise up within me. I felt as though I would drown in my sorrow.

After awhile I began to cry all those tears I'd had inside of me for so long—not just for the loss of Randy but also for the twenty-six years of abandonment, rejection, and loneliness I'd felt throughout my life. I sobbed for the frightened little girl, the lonely teenager, and the insecure woman I'd become. I cried for every single hurt I'd experienced in my life. I cried until there were no more tears. This was the lowest point of my life.

What I had feared most had happened: Randy had abandoned me. The stark realization sparked a thread of insanity inside of me. My state of mind as a love addict was best described by author, Pia Mellody, "Their partners . . . abandoned them for someone or some-thing. . . . The love addict's drug, the partner, is now withdrawn. . . . Original feelings of childhood abandonment are activated along with adult feelings about the current abandonment . . . trigger experiences ranging from feeling depressed to feeling suicidal. The fear . . . can range from frustration to feeling rageful and perhaps homicidal."[5]

Just as the book described, I didn't want to breathe anymore; but in the middle of my madness, that survival instinct I'd learned as a child welled up inside of me, and the tears poured out of me. Around two o'clock in the morning I drug myself off the floor. There were no more tears. With little regard for the lateness of the hour, I picked up the telephone and called my therapist, Dr. Doctor.

With a great resolve, I wanted to tell him that I had to get well. I longed to be married and have a healthy relationship like a normal person. I wanted to plead, "Can you help me?" But there was a message stating that Dr. Doctor was out of town. I felt abandoned even by him.

Never had I felt such despair. Just like the woman in Proverbs 14:1, I had torn my house down with my own hands. It was time for me to face the person I had become. Throwing a few things in a bag, I jumped into my car and drove all the way to Colorado. I was desperate to find love. This time I found it in my mom and John. They were totally there for me. It was a huge thing for me to know I had a safe place to go . . . and this time it wasn't into another man's arms. They nurtured and loved me back to as much emotional stability as I was capable of having at this point in my life. I stayed there for a month until I felt well enough to face my demons, and then I went home.

Chapter 13

Alone Again

Who you are speaks so loudly
I cannot hear what you say.

—Ralph Waldo Emerson

Randy had moved back into our home while I was in Colorado. When I was ready to come back, he agreed to let me stay there until I could get on my feet and we could sell the house.

Once I was back, one of Randy's friends called to ask me to leave the house so Randy could come and pick up his things. Although I found comfort in having his things around, I couldn't forestall the inevitable any longer, so I agreed. Randy came and moved out everything he owned. Returning to the half-empty house, I was now void of any shred of hope. As empty as the house felt, my soul felt emptier.

The divorce proceedings continued, but I left him literally hundreds of psychotic messages and sent him lengthy passionate letters professing my undying love to him. He ignored every single one of them. Later I'd feel humiliated and wish I could call back and erase the messages.

I really didn't want to live anymore, not without Randy. The thought of losing him, his family, and my home was devastating. His mom sensed my fragility and agreed to lend me $10,000 so I could buy Randy out of our house. She was intuitive enough to know that it was important to my sanity for me to keep the house. I needed that stability to help me survive this crisis. I promised to repay her, and she said, "Set your own terms, but I have one condition—that when you repay me, you bring the money to me in person because I want to see you again." It was comforting to know that losing Randy didn't mean I had to lose his mother's friendship or my home.

Slowly I began to put the pieces of my life back together. I was going to auditions, doing some guest-star appearances on television shows, and working in a few commercials. I was also in an acting class. I was getting by, but I was in constant pain over the loss of Randy. Every time I booked a job I'd call him, believing that if I became a famous actress he'd want me back.

I had to pick myself up. Subsequently I refinanced the house in order to reduce my payments, and then I rented my sister a room. Soon I got a third roommate to help cover my expenses, which lifted a lot of the financial pressure from my shoulders. Faithful Mr. Feffer was there to pick up the pieces for me again. Sadly, I couldn't respect Bob for allowing himself to be used by me. Guys always say girls don't like nice guys; they only like jerks. The reality is girls don't respect suckers.

On the positive side I was seeing the therapist, Dr. Doctor, on a regular basis, and he was beginning to address a myriad of my problems.

My mom as a teen after winning a beauty contest.

My mom and dad's wedding—1964.

Me at 18 months—early 1975.

Me and my sister Kristine at the house in Florida before my parents divorced.

Family trip to California—Mom, Kristine, Dad, Me, and of course the dogs.

*My mom's parents and the only
grandparents I would know —
Nana and Pop-Pop.*

*Trip with Nana and Pop-Pop —
(l to r) Pop-Pop, Robin, Nana, my
cousin Eric, me, and Kristine.*

*My 9th birthday at Nana and
Pop-Pop's house. (l to r) Eric, Nana,
John, me, and my friend Jennifer.*

*Me showing one of Mom's dogs in the
Parade of Champions — 1976.*

*Me, my stepfather John,
and my mom.*

Me riding Robin's horse Annie.
I loved to ride bareback.

Me and my horse Chandy after winning our
first blue ribbon — 1984.

The ranch in Elizabeth,
Colorado.

Graduation from Ponderosa
High School — 1988.

I was in the chorus in the play Greese my
sophomore year in high school — 1986.

My Uncle Don and Aunt Sheri and my cousins, Kim, Nicky, and Russel. This picture was taken just before I moved in with them in 1988.

Kristine, Mom, and me with our horse, Conrade. This was when Bob Feffer and I went back to Colorado to buy the horse—1991.

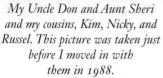

Our first house together—Me, Rob, and our dog Buster.

My dad, me, and Rob in Florida visiting my dad. Rob asked him for my hand—1998.

My 29th birthday—Robin, Chauncey, Heather, Brenda, Scott and me.

My good friend Chris Chauncey and I. Chauncey was a great Christian example — 1998.

Location shoot for Sunset Beach — 1998.

Rob and I going to the Soap Opera Digest Awards when I was on Sunset Beach — 1998. (photo by John Paschal)

My wedding day wearing the necklace and head piece Robin made for me — 1999.

Our favorite wedding photo.

The day the doctor confirmed I was pregnant!

Kyle and I in my dressing room at The Bold and the Beautiful. My mom watched Kyle while I worked—2001.

Me and my mom at photo shoot for The Bold and the Beautiful. The photo appeared in the Soap Opera Digest Mother's Day issue—2001. (photo by Leslie Brown)

Kyle and I the day we shot The Bold and the Beautiful cast photo—2001.

My stepfather John and my son Kyle, at age 1.

Rob and I on the ranch.
(photo by John Paschal)

Me, Kyle, and Buster out for
an afternoon walk.

Good friends from our church — (l to r)
Camie, me, Aiden, and Kyle, age 2.
Aiden and Kyle are best buddies.
Camie is the wife of one of the guys
Rob works with. We have become
great friends. We all attend church
together and Aiden and Kyle were
dedicated the same Sunday.

Robin, Kristine, Mom, Nana, me, Robin's
daughter Brianna, and Kyle — 2002.

My beautiful son Kyle — age 3.

Chandy's son now is the one who carried me to the winners circle. Me and Dozar winning The Championship—2004. (photo by Locke Photography)

Kyle and I riding our horse Dozar, one of Chandy's offspring—2004.

Kyle showing Dozar at a horse show—2004.

Rob, Kyle, and I at Kristine's house. We enjoy spending time with her and her family—2004.

Because I couldn't live and breathe without a man in my life, I couldn't wait until I got well but believed I quickly had to find a substitute for Randy. Every night I was out running around and looking for love in all the wrong places. I started by telephoning every man who had ever been in my life.

Bob Feffer was already at the scene to help me pick up the pieces of my life. Since my house had a yard with a pool, he showed me how to take care of it and clean the pool myself to save money. Bob also fixed everything that broke. There was nothing between us other than a deep friendship. So my search continued.

Thinking of all the men who had been in my life, I decided to call the number one man on my list, the well-known actor. To my surprise, he rebuffed me. I assume that because I was no longer married, I wasn't safe for him anymore.

Next I phoned Kent, the guy I'd met on the movie set the first time I filmed a movie of the week. I attempted to rekindle my film location romance with him. There was a real freedom and comfort level being with Kent. I felt safe with him, and he never put any demands on me.

On what would have been our fourth anniversary, Randy surprised me and showed up at our house. This was exactly what I longed for every night. I didn't even know where he lived or what his number was. All I had was a pager number; he wanted nothing to do with me. The more I tried to reach out to him, the farther he would run, and now he was at my door.

I wasn't at home, but unfortunately Kent was. I never knew why Randy stopped by my house that day. I felt a mixture of anger, rage, and sadness, but I could never get any kind of response from him about why he came by to see me. I was tormented by thoughts of why he had come. Had he planned to tell me he wanted to make another go of things? Whatever plans or hopes Randy had were deminished when he came by our home and Kent opened the door. To this day, I still don't know what Randy wanted.

I would never know the answer to that. Instead of trusting my circumstances and God's sovereignty, once again I was making bad choices just to help numb the pain of my loss and aloneness. Although it was the desire of my heart to be with Randy, instead of waiting patiently for him to come around, my desire to have a man in my life ruled, and I had replaced him with Kent. Instead of being honorable, I blew my last chance of mending fences with Randy. I was bummed, but at least I wasn't alone; I had Kent in my life. At last this crisis had finally triggered a plea for help from me.

Dr. Doctor became my lifeline, and because I had excellent insurance, I was able to see him frequently. Once I began opening up to the psychiatrist, I was able to shed some of the layers of abuse in my life. He began explaining why I was suffering from intense emotional pain. Like my mother, I had become a relationship addict. In her book *Women Who Love Too Much* Robin Norwood defines a woman like me as a "man junkie," strung out on pain, fear, and yearning. She further stated, "We use relationships in the same way that we use our addictive substance: to take our pain away."[6] Going through my divorce was like a heroin addict going through withdrawal. As I was forced to withdraw from my relationship with Randy, I numbed the pain with Kent.

Dealing with my pain, I sat in the therapist's office several times a week as he adeptly helped me to overcome my overwhelming addiction for men. Dr. Doctor also pointed out that a relationship addict lived like an alcoholic, crazy for her next drink. Instead of alcohol, he pointed out that my drug of choice was a man.

One day following therapy, I asked myself, *Do you really want a relationship with a guy who slept with me when I was married? No!* I knew I would never have a serious relationship with someone

I didn't respect, and I knew deep down he had no respect for me either. I was a cheater. I allowed my relationship with Kent to fizzle out.

Although I was alone again, an intolerable place for me to be, I was getting healthier, thanks to Dr. Doctor. He explained the only way out of pain is through it, not around it. He was forcing me to face my circumstances instead of avoiding them. One day the doctor forced me to look in the mirror and take a good look at myself. I didn't like what I saw. I knew the time had come for me to make a commitment to work on myself. *Because if anyone is a hearer of the word and not a doer, he is like a man looking at his own face in a mirror; for he looks at himself, goes away, and right away forgets what kind of man he was (James 1:23–24).*

This look in the mirror was a turning point for me. I began journaling and reading stacks and stacks of self-help books. Without a man in my life, I was ashamed to admit that the only thing that was holding me together was the hope there might be another man somewhere out there for me. Dr. Doctor assured me that no man that was worthy would be interested in me until first I'd done some intensive work.

Dr. Doctor was sympathetic, helping me build my self-esteem so I would no longer require a male's approval and have the hope of being in a healthy relationship. During one therapy session, I told my doctor how much I missed riding motorcycles. He smiled and said, "Why don't you buy one?"

I'd never thought of it. I'd always believed that I needed a man to ride with, but I did some research and took his advice. I even talked my friend Heather, who was also going through a divorce, into buying one too. We were two angry females on motorcycles. You should have seen Heather and me tooling around L.A. on our bikes, two blonde babes speeding down the highway. We both loved the freedom of the open road, and I was never concerned about safety because truthfully, I didn't really care if I lived or died. My life had no value to me because I felt no one valued me.

It was more than the freedom and the enjoyment. In the past, I had always believed that I needed a guy to ride a motorcycle. Now I had stepped out of the box, gotten a license, and bought a motorcycle. This was an epiphany for me. This realization freed me from a lot of my hang-ups and took me one step closer to being healed of my relationship addiction. I learned a difficult lesson that was really so simple: I needed to give myself what I was demanding others to give me.

As time passed and my therapy continued, I became less willing to take any more life-threatening risks. This was a huge time of growth for me. I was looking for *something more*. Unfortunately, I was still trying to find it in all the wrong places. I replayed the tapes of our marriage over and over in my mind. All the things that Randy had said about me in the heat of an argument rolled around in my head: "You're so Hollywood; you'd do anything to be a famous actress."

Maybe Randy was right. I'd give the Hollywood scene a try. I'd always dreamed of the glamorous life. I'd also heard of the trendy Hollywood clubs, the hangouts of the rich and famous, so my girlfriend and I got dressed up and hit Sunset Boulevard. While we were standing outside in a long line that stretched halfway around the block, a refined, well-dressed gentleman approached us.

"How would you girls like to go to the front of the line?"

We looked at each other and then at the meandering line and replied, "Sure."

Our charming host, David, ushered us inside and seated us at the table of one of Hollywood's most famous producers. We were excited. This move had to be good for my career. One of the other women at the table confided in me that David was bankrolled by some of the top producers and directors in the industry who enjoyed being surrounded by beautiful starlets for an evening. Sounded like a pimp to me, but I didn't care. I was footloose, fancy-free, and miserable. I wanted a taste of the good life. I deserved it, didn't I?

Before David excused himself, he handed me one of his cards and winked. "You're too pretty to stand in lines. The next time you want to go out, give me a call."

I grabbed the card and tucked it into my evening bag. After a thrilling evening with the famous producer, I decided to give David a call for another glamorous evening. Away from that red-neck country girl and into the glitz of a Hollywood babe, night after night, I began to fool around in Satan's playground with the powerful, rich, and famous.

I was going to all the nicest restaurants and hanging out with the A list. Bankrolled by his wealthy clients, David even supplied the money for expensive clothes, hair, and makeup since it was important for the girls to look glamorous on their nights out on the town.

Mistakenly, I believed that my newly discovered Hollywood activities might provide the big break in my career, but when I asked one of the better known directors if there really was such a thing as the "casting couch," he replied cynically.

"Baby, we sure want you to think there is, but you'd better believe that when I have millions of dollars, plus my business and my reputation on the line with a film, there's no woman worth that."

Respecting my boldness and intelligence, this man later became a personal friend of mine.

Going out with these powerful men, I was having a blast until a few of the guys started coming on too strong. I got into a couple of inappropriate situations, and feeling like I owed these men something for the clothes and the nice restaurants, I didn't refuse their advances. I was terribly ashamed of my behavior and wanted out of this debauched lifestyle. I was sinking fast, and if I didn't get out, I knew that I might never escape.

One weekend a top producer in town had seen me around and specifically requested me as his escort for an evening. He would be a great connection for me, but my heart belonged to country dancing, and when I heard that Rhett Akins was performing at Borderline Country Club, I much preferred to go see Rhett.

Consequently, I said no to the producer and began to pull away from this whole decadent Hollywood scene. At times you have to go as far away from who you are to realize where you belong. This was truly not the life for me. In spite of what Randy said, I was just a country girl at heart.

Because of my experiences, I'll never wonder about glamorous life. It's not what it's cracked up to be. You get a lot of special treatment. And there were great perks; you get to dress up in designer clothes and go to all the nice restaurants and clubs. Anything you needed or wanted these guys made sure you got, but besides that it's a pretty empty existence. Eventually I traded the Hollywood moguls for the dating scene once again.

At this same time I was enrolled in an acting class taught by Larry Moss, a renowned drama coach. While studying with him, I heard his name lauded from the Academy podium on Oscar night. I felt proud to be in his class and hung onto his every word.

On his recommended reading list was a book called *The Artist's Way*. It came with *The Morning Pages Journal* that advocated a specific way of journaling. First thing in the morning, the journalist is supposed to write three pages in longhand in the journal. I mentioned in one of my entries that I felt like it was more the *Morning Rages*. I had so much anger pouring out of me.

In class we learned various relaxation techniques to use when auditioning or acting. Following our exercises one evening,

Larry Moss asked us to pull out our journal to free associate. "Start answering this question and don't edit yourself. Keep writing until I say stop. The question I want you to answer is, why do you want to be an actor?"

I still have the notebook. This is exactly what I wrote: "Love, acceptance, validation, attention, respect, power, to be heard, money, revenge, fear of failure, revenge, to prove to everyone that I could, it is a success everyone will know I had. I want everyone to be sorry they weren't more kind to me, to stick it to everyone who hurt me. I feel I have something to say! Something to offer! To be heard, to be seen, to create, to teach people from my experience, to express my insight, to feel, to fantasize, to play, to be angry, to fantasize, to play, to explore, to be sexy, to be appreciated."

Through this journaling I had an epiphany. Is vengence a good motivation for how you live your life? After that class I developed a new resolve to get on with my life. That same evening one of my fellow students approached me. She said she was a New Age follower. There are thousands of New Agers in California who believe that you can be your own god and make things happen. Confiding my troubles to her, I told her I was desperately trying to get over Randy. She said she thought she could help me, so she loaned me a copy of a New Age philosophical book to read. She also mentioned that the book contained several strong principles of the universe. One of these principles immediately piqued my interest, "Believe it will be there, and it will be."

This God stuff sounded pretty good to me, but before I attacked my big request for Randy to come home, I decided to start small. I was in terrible financial trouble, so I stepped out in a childlike faith and believed that my mortgage payment was miraculously going to appear in my mailbox before the due date.

The formula worked perfectly. Literally the day before the payment was due, I opened my mailbox, and there was a check from a TV show rerun of the movie from the week with Robert Conrad in the right amount. Wow!

I couldn't wait to go to therapy to tell Dr. Doctor about the epiphany I had in my acting class. I told him I wanted to change my life. I no longer wanted to be the person I was anymore. "I want to marry again."

"What kind of man do you see yourself with, Tracy?"

I described a man with strong integrity, honor, and character. When I finished, I thought the doctor would be proud of me, but his response surprised me. "That kind of man would never marry a girl like you."

"Why not?"

"Because you are too insecure, too immature, and far too needy."

At first I was offended but I knew he was right. "I don't want to be that girl anymore. I want to be the kind of woman that kind of man would want to marry."

The doctor smiled. "Well, we have a lot of work to do to make you that kind of man's ideal woman."

"Where do we begin?" I asked.

"If you want to move forward, you must build a foundation."

"How do I do that?"

"I want you to start investigating religions and find a faith that can help you build a foundation. Your lack of parental dependence in your life forced you to look for it in other places, in men. This male dependence has strangled your development and kept your maturation process on hold. You have the maturity of a ten-year-old."

"That's exactly the age I was when my grandfather died and my grandmother kicked my sister and me out of the house," I reminded him.

Instead of offering me any self-pity, he continued. "When you couldn't find love at home, you went looking for it. You found your self-worth in a relationship with a man at barely fourteen. Now everything in your life centers on a man. I want you to transfer this dependency from man to God. I want you to learn how to depend on God."

What wisdom this man had! He didn't recommend that I try any particular religion, but he said it was imperative that I find something to believe in that wouldn't disappointment me. He further explained that there was no way I could get better without a foundation.

Having just experienced a kernel of a miracle of faith with my rent check through the girlfriend in acting class, I was more than open to his suggestion. I admitted that I knew nothing about God, but I made a commitment that I would find out. Although I know now that this book did not contain the truth, I believe that God used it to soften and prepare my heart for him. I was off on a quest for God.

I kept track of these God moments in my journal. God was surrounding me with people who each provided a piece in the puzzle for my salvation. It's amazing how he can often even use people who aren't Christians. The Lord is wooing us to him through people and circumstances.

Prior to a crusade in Atlanta, evangelist Billy Graham explained this best. Dr. Graham said it usually takes at least forty people to lead a person to the Lord. The first person thinks they did nothing; the last person thinks they did everything. They're both wrong. It is God who did it. He is the One who arranged the divine appointments for those forty people to contribute to a person's salvation. This was certainly true in my life.

One of these divine appointments in my life was my acting class. In addition to the couple of people who helped prompt my spiritual awakening by giving me books, God put in my life a couple of other people who were Christians. One was Chris Chauncey; she became my closest friend in the class and was the person who came to my rescue when things fell apart with Randy. I called her Chauncey since I have a sister named Kris. She and her boyfriend Scott, also a Christian, joined my acting class, the three of us became instant friends. They broke up shortly afterward, but we all remained friends.

During my divorce Chauncey was there, but I shut her out a lot because I knew of her faith, and I felt shame over my behavior. I was angry, so I was acting out, exhibiting psychotic behavior; and though I was legally still married, I was seeing other men. Because she was a Christian, I fully expected her to judge me, but this was how little I understood Christianity. Unbeknownst to me, she had been praying for me all long. The two of them would often offer me mild introductions to Jesus Christ. Instead of preaching to me, they subtly mentioned how God was working in their lives. I made notes in my journal of how God was working in my own life.

As I flipped through the pages, I noted that the changes in my life were reflected in my journal. At the beginning of 1996, I started my journal. Sadly, this was near the same time when Randy's accident occurred. Things seemed to be going well in our marriage when suddenly all that changed. I can't totally blame the accident because I'm sure that had it not occurred I would have done something else stupid myself to destroy our marriage.

Initially, I used the name of God in my journal, without even capitalizing his name. It is fascinating to read my journal, for God went from a general term used almost like slang. In August of that same year as Chauncey and Scott continued to plant seeds about Jesus Christ in their conversation with me, I began to capitalize his name.

One day in April, I was venting to Chauncey at her apartment. I recorded those same words I relayed to her in my journal on April 23, 1997:

> *I hate this feeling. I wake up feeling so uneasy. I am not even sure what the feeling is; it's just something's not right. It's a guilty feeling, like I am doing something wrong. I feel like I woke up and suddenly realized that I'd overslept and I had this big important thing I missed. There's something I am supposed to be doing. I went to extreme measures my entire life to avoid this pain and was quite proud of the fact that no one had ever gotten to me. I also used to feel superior because I never needed glasses or braces on my teeth. Now I need both. I guess I am being humbled. God, I'm in so much pain—I feel like my life no longer has meaning or purpose.*

When I expressed these same feelings to Chauncey, she asked me if I believed in God.

Did I believe in God? I had to stop and think about it.

"I suppose I believe there is a God," I replied, but then I added my usual junk. "But I don't believe in organized religion, so I don't go to church. I don't think you need to go to church to talk to God."

"What is your God based on then?" she asked me.

I had no answer. No one had ever asked me that question. I had never put an identity on God. He was just this imaginary friend that I made into whatever or whomever I wanted or needed him to be at the time. I brought God around when it was convenient.

Chauncey excused herself and disappeared into her room. A few minutes later she came back carrying her Bible. Bless her heart, here was this beautiful woman who had won countless beauty pageants and other awards, sitting beside me and reading me Bible verses. The verse I remember so well is found in Matthew 12:30, which says: *Anyone who is not with Me is against Me, and anyone who does not gather with Me scatters.* Chauncey continued to explain to me that per this verse, it is impossible to be neutral in Christ. Anyone who is not actively following him has chosen to reject him.

"How did you find all that out? I asked.

"I've read the Bible in its entirety twice. All the answers to your problems are right here." She pointed to the Bible.

I admired Chauncey for that accomplishment. Knowledge has always given me a sense of comfort and power. If what she said was true, that all the answers were in there, I was intrigued by the Book but not enough to run out and buy one. I still had a self-centered way of basing things solely on my feelings and didn't feel that I necessarily needed a crutch like the Bible.

"Look up for the answers," Chauncey advised me. "Don't try to figure it out in your head."

From that point on, when I was talking to Chauncey or Scott about my situation, especially my divorce, they would both reference the Bible. Scott even bought me my first Bible for Christmas that year. Chauncey and Scott would follow up with me and ask if I had read a particular passage. The two of them walked me through the Bible. I looked through it like Charlie Chaplin, "looking for a loophole."

I began to pray humbly, my pathetic pleas to God, to bring Randy home. It didn't change things because God doesn't violate man's free will. My friend Chauncey told me that the Lord can move in a man's heart, but it's the man who controls the outcome of his actions. Accepting this was difficult for me. Childishly I wanted to pray to a god who would make Randy do what I wanted him to do.

Had I married the wrong person? Perhaps God had someone else out there for me? Naturally, having a man in my life was a much higher priority for me than God. *Do not have other gods besides Me (Exod. 20:3)*. I'd broken this commandment more than once. Men were my gods; whoever happened to be the man in my life was the god I served.

As I was writing a letter to God in my journal, I felt that he spoke to my heart. I wouldn't find a man until I was ready to receive the man that God had for me, a man who would be an extension of God's love for me. I wasn't ready to make a commitment, but having God to talk to was beginning to make a difference in my life.

My only problem was that I didn't know God well enough to fully trust him, and I wasn't convinced enough to seek him so that I could learn to trust him.

Chapter 14

A Divine Appointment

God knew his chosen time:
He bade me slowly ripen to my prime,
And from my boughs withheld the promised fruit,
Till storm and sun gave vigor to the root.

—BAYARD TAYLOR, *Possession*

Although less and less frequent, on occasion I would find myself back on the Randy channel. One of the things I missed most about Randy was dancing with him. Never before had I danced with anyone like him. Through my therapy I finally realized I could still dance even if it wasn't with him. Instead of staying home alone and having a pity party, I'd go out to a country bar to escape my loneliness and throw myself into one of my favorite pastimes, dancing at a honky-tonk. How freeing it was to cut the rug and listen to the music.

On one occasion I actually ran into Randy and his new girl-friend at the Borderline, one of my dancing hangouts. Sooner or later it was bound to happen, and I had tried to prepare myself for the inevitable. Ironically, I had dreamed of this happening months before it actually did. I think God was preparing me.

Fortunately, the night I saw them my dance card was full, and I was having a great time. When I turned around, I caught a glimpse of Randy and Ann sitting at a table. I was truly shocked at how shameful they both looked when they saw me. *You can have him!* I thought to myself. I realized that I didn't want him anymore. I wanted the man and the marriage that I had described to Dr. Doctor.

With the same passion I had once put in finding a man, I concentrated on getting well. I threw myself into therapy. At my acting coach's recommendation, I was reading self-help books including *Facing Love Addiction* written by Pia Mellody, *Your Erroneous Zones* by Dr. Wayne Dyer, John Bradshaw's *Homecoming*, and a stack more.

Along with my friends Chauncey and Scott, who had recently moved to the West Coast and didn't yet have a church home, I began to visit churches in the area. My conversations with Chauncey and Scott were becoming more and more Christ focused, and I was reading the Bible that Scott had given me. I began to say the word *God* without whispering when I was in public. I was coming out of the closet, so to speak.

For the first time in my life, I was consciously trying to obey God. I also was trying to trust in God's plan for my life. Beginning to believe there was a plan and a reason for everything, I penned these thoughts about my future in my journal, "My next husband is still out there somewhere, and I know that God will give him to me when I am ready to receive him."

I changed my focus from wanting Randy to wanting to become the right spouse for the right husband. Looking up to the heavens at night, I would talk to God. Although I didn't know his name, I would also talk to my future husband concerning the plans and dreams I had for our future. It was what I would later learn is an act of faith. I knew this intuitively, not scripturally. I was thanking God in advance. When I started to give up the control of my life, my life began to improve. I wasn't committed to Christ, but the Holy Spirit was working mightily in me.

The next time I went to the Borderline, I wasn't looking for a man, but I was there strictly because I enjoyed dancing. I met Eric, a guy who subsequently became my friend and partner. A great dancer, Eric knew how to do all the flips and dips, and he was an extraordinary swing dancer—as good if not better than Randy. Life went on. We began to meet on a regular basis to dance together.

It was so great for me to find someone who enjoyed my hobby as much as I did but who also wasn't interested in a relationship with me. When it comes to two-step and swing, the woman is only as good as her partner since he leads.

"How about a change of scenery?" Eric suggested one night. Night after night we'd danced to the same music with the same crowd, so I agreed it might be fun.

"There's a new bar I've heard about that I want to try," Eric replied. "It's kind of far away."

"If you'll drive, I'll go." I agreed, and we set a date for November 22, a day I'll never forget.

While I was getting ready for our date, I was listening to the song "I Wanna Fall in Love" by Lila McCann. I turned up the radio and sang the song like a prayer. Eric hadn't shown up. Finally he showed up at nine o'clock, apologizing profusely. Eric was in the military, stationed at Port Magu in Oxnard, and had gotten delayed at the base.

We left my house a lot later than we planned, and by ten o'clock, halfway there, Eric noticed I was yawning, so he asked me if I was going to be able to make it.

"I am kind of tired," I admitted. "I know of this other place called The Western Connection that's right up here. How about if we stop here for a while, and if you don't like it, I'll go with you to the other place. If you do, we'll just stay here tonight and try The Midnight Rodeo another time."

"Deal," Eric agreed.

When we went inside The Western Connection, the bouncer refused to let Eric inside because he wasn't wearing a collared shirt. Obviously, our heavenly Father takes care of all the details. Eric just happened to have a shirt in his truck and went out to grab it, but I chose not to venture out again in the cold night air.

Waiting for Eric to return from his truck, I turned around, when all of a sudden, in walks the most beautiful man I'd ever seen. He was clad in a pair of tight-fitting Wrangler jeans and a cowboy hat. Either you get it or you don't, but there is something about a man in a cowboy hat. The sight of him took my breath away. "There he is," my heart sang out. This man was the picture of the husband I'd imagined in my mind all of my life. In the past, each guy I'd meet was a part of what I wanted or needed, but this guy embodied all my dreams. *Is he the one?*

At that same moment the words of Karen and Richard Carpenter's song "Close to Me" played in my mind as the handsome hunk moved across the floor: "Why do birds suddenly appear each time when you're near?" The background blurred, and he was in slow motion as he disappeared into the crowd.

Eric returned, dressed in a collared shirt, and he and I took a spin on the dance floor until he spotted a girl he liked. The two of them ran off together on the dance floor and left me standing alone like a dork. I tried to appear cool and inconspicuous. After all, this could be Mr. Right nearby. I'd look around and bob my head to the music trying to find him in the crowd.

After a few songs, I finally spotted him standing over by the bar, surrounded by a group of guys. In an effort to get his attention, I pretended I had to go the ladies room and sashayed right past him. Nothing. I came out of the restroom and went back to dancing with Eric again. Despite my attempts to catch the stranger's eye, he never looked my way. *Maybe it's this ponytail.* Hadn't everyone told me my hair was my best feature? I excused myself to Eric and ran back to the ladies room and took my hair down. It tumbled down to my shoulders, and I fluffed it up all around my face.

I went back out and strained to see if the guy was wearing a wedding ring. Good! There was no ring, but he didn't notice seem to notice me. I passed by again, but this time with my hair down. Still nothing. I had to go to plan B.

Boldly I went right up to the bar and stood next to him and was trying to get the bartender's attention. Heart pounding, I stood there like a loser.

"What are you waiting for?" the handsome stranger asked me.

His words stung me like a burr. I took his comment to mean, what are you doing here; go away. I told him I was trying to order a Coke.

Immediately, he called out to the waitress, "Debbie, can you get this girl a Coke?"

Oh no, this waitress must be his girlfriend, I thought.

Although the handsome hunk ignored me, he insisted on paying for my Coke, but I assumed this is where it would all end. I thanked him and sat down at a table. No one seemed to notice me, and no one approached me to ask me to dance. I felt invisible until I looked up to see the stranger walking toward me.

"I'm a little confused here," he admitted. "Is that guy you came in with your boyfriend?"

"No," I smiled. "Is Debbie your girlfriend?"

"Nope," he replied with a grin. "May I sit down?"

I kicked out a chair and thought, *God bless this dear man for coming up to me to clear the air.* What a gentleman! Most people who go to country bars are there to dance so they don't pay any attention to the partner who brought you, but not Rob. He was more interested in getting to know me, not just to dance with me. My therapist was teaching me how to recognize a quality guy, and I knew immediately that this guy was indeed a quality guy.

We chatted for fifteen minutes. He told me his name was Rob and that he was a police officer. I said, "My dad's a police officer."

I was thinking, *Wow a cowboy and a cop! He's like all the village people in one.*

We chatted about my dad and then he asked, "Would you like to dance later?"

I nodded yes, and then he got up and left. I did some line dancing. Yeah, by now I had given in and learned the dances. Then he finally came up to me and asked me to dance. We danced, and then he left again. This guy wasn't clingy at all, and according to my therapist, this was a healthy thing. A lot of guys think if they even buy you a Coke that you owe them and they own you in a sense, but Rob was different. From the first night he let me know I owed him nothing and I wasn't obligated to him. We visited once and danced once.

After our dance Eric came over and said, "We've got a long drive, Tracy. We should go."

I walked over to Rob to tell him I was leaving, and he asked for my number. I, of course, gave it to him and forced myself to leave.

Saturday came and went, and Rob hadn't called me. I was bummed. All sorts of doubts were going through my head. *He didn't like me. He lost my phone number. He's married.*

I began to pray that he would call me, but Sunday passed and then by the end of the day on Monday, there was still no phone call. I wasn't breathing. Waiting was excruciating for this recovering relationship addict. In the past I'd been such a manipulative control freak, I had to convince myself not to call the LAPD and hunt Rob down like the impulsive psycho I used to be. By now I had learned that God was in control, not me and to trust his sovereignty. If this guy is the one, God would bring him into my life again.

By Monday I began to loose hope, so that night I went to a sports bar with a friend to watch *Monday Night Football,* hoping to distract myself. Yet I couldn't wait to get home to check my messages. As soon as I walked in the door, I glanced at my answering machine. It was blinking. Rob had called, and he left his number. I didn't wait. I was dialing as he was saying his number on the machine. Perhaps I still was a little impulsive.

Rob and I chatted amicably for a while, and then he finally got around to asking me out for the next Friday night. I loved how he wasn't smothering. OK, a part of me wasn't used to it, but it was good for me to pause and remember to take my time. *Don't rush the relationship.*

On Friday afternoon I had a horse show at the L.A. Equestrian Center, so I asked Rob to pick me up there. On our first date he took me out to dinner. He let me pick the restaurant since he lived fifty miles away. I chose The Wood Ranch.

I thought Friday night would never come. Rob picked me up in a pickup truck. Things were looking good. This is just the kind of vehicle that appeals to a country girl with a horse. We drove to The Wood Ranch, a nice restaurant with country flair.

Truthfully, it didn't matter where we were since we were enjoying talking so much. The more we talked and the more I knew about him, the more excited I got that God had put meaning into my suffering and blessed me again. My divorce seemed like the worst thing in the world to me, and I couldn't understand why it had to happen. Now in the first hours I'd spent with Rob, I was beginning to understand why.

God used my suffering to teach me the lessons I needed to learn before I could enter into a healthy relationship. Prior to this I would not have been the kind of woman that a man of Rob's character would want in his life.

I will never forget when we were walking back to his truck. He actually asked if he could hold my hand. What a pleasant change! We had a mutual respect for each other. I squeezed his hand and never wanted to let it go.

After we got in the truck, I just stared at his beautiful, strong hand in mine. I knew without a doubt that I could love this man and it was an even playing field—no one rescuing or picking up someone's broken pieces. Mature adults who didn't *need* to be together but *wanted* to be. We had such a good time that he came back on Saturday and saw me show my horse. He asked me out for the next weekend, and we began to date every weekend and on Wednesday night too.

My relationship with Rob was the only healthy relationship I'd ever experienced. Unlike most of the men I'd dated, Rob didn't try to impress me, nor did he pretend to be someone he was not. Rob was just Rob, and truthfully through my therapy, Tracy had become just Tracy. I refused to play the role of the femme fatale and try to get Rob to fall for me. I was not going to try and control him either.

After our first date there were no professions of love, nor did a dozen roses appear at my door. While these things can be impressive, it's not a sign of true love. We wanted to take things slow so our relationship would take root. We didn't have to spend every moment together but remained independent. We loved our time together but didn't give up our friends, our responsibilities, and our hobbies as I had done many times in the past. At the same time, as the days passed, we both knew what we meant to each other and where we stood.

I knew that ultimately I wanted to spend the rest of my life with Rob. But this time I was going to approach it the right way. I prayed that I wouldn't mess things up or sabotage this relationship.

Chapter 15

A New Love and a New Heart

*Nothing moves a woman so deeply as the
boyhood of the man she loves.*

—ANNIE DILLARD, *The Living*

With Rob I was experiencing a healthy relationship for the first time in my life. Being in a mature relationship doesn't happen instantly. I had to monitor myself closely. It takes a commitment. I had to take the time to consider the consequences of my actions before I reacted. In the past I became so enraged when I felt unloved by someone it would result in my throwing a major temper tantrum. I would try to force them to pay attention to me or to love me. In doing so, I became less lovable and therefore got the opposite of what I so wanted. It is a vicious cycle. I would ask myself, *Is this wise? What is the cost, and what is the payoff?*

I also learned to be honest about my true intentions for all of my actions. Am I doing this to make him feel guilty or to express a righteous need? Staying in therapy, I wanted to prevent myself from destroying this relationship. I was like an alcoholic visiting a bar again, and I needed the support of my therapist. Rob was supportive of my therapy and even went with me on some of my visits to Dr. Doctor. I needed my doctor's approval to feel confident that I was not choosing my greatest fear but my greatest love.

Rob was a man in every sense of the word. When I would begin a destructive cycle, he would tell me, "That's on you." He never allowed me to hold him accountable for the pain of my past, and I would sometimes get furious and think he must not love me. Then I would realize that those wrongs were not his debt to pay. While my therapist cautioned me to take it slow, I think he was genuinely pleased that I was seeing a man of Rob's character.

Getting to know Rob was like going on an adventure. A California native, Rob lived about an hour from me out in the Inland Empire area. When he first took me there to meet his partner, I adored the area. He told me that a lot of his friends from work lived out there. One of my favorite things about driving there was the scenery of rolling green hills with cows grazing; it reminded me of my home in Colorado. This town wasn't pretentious at all but a true suburbia with tons of churches, schools, and clean streets.

The son of a police officer, Rob was a local jock who went on to play football for Orange Coast Junior College. At six feet two inches, Rob was tall and handsome. He exhibited that clean-cut police officer image, and of course he had a mustache. Upon graduation he entered the police academy, and afterward he'd joined the Los Angeles Police Department where he worked hard and was promoted to Metro. From there he rose within the ranks to the SWAT team, the most elite platoon in the Metro Division. And there it was—I read on his SWAT T-shirt everything I had told Dr. Doctor I wanted in a man: uncompromised duty, honor, and valor. How great is that? A sign that even I couldn't miss— there is a God!

Rob even told me he had never taken a sick day at work. This told me that he was reliable, and since I had been robbed of having reliable people in my life, this was the quality I admired most. I was so blessed that this man in a uniform had a strong attraction to me.

We also connected on a deeper level. The similarities between our lives were startling. Rob had suffered a somewhat traumatic childhood too. Similar to my parents, his mother and father had also been high school sweethearts who had gotten pregnant as teenagers with Rob's older sister Dawn. Two years later Rob came along. After a series of affairs, Rob's father left his mother for another woman; and they, like my parents, divorced when Rob was only two years old.

Like my father, Rob's father was also a police officer. So many times in my life a policeman had come to my rescue. No wonder I was in love with one. Beginning with Wally Wessel, the local sheriff in Elizabeth; then the two cops who saved my life when Randy and I fought; and now my Rob, the most wonderful cop of all.

Rob's parents' divorce had a profound effect on their son's life. Vowing he would never marry young and end up like his folks, he wanted to wait until he was mature enough to understand and honor the commitment he was making. From his father's experience as a police officer, he was well acquainted with the stress of the job and how it changes a man. He wanted first to discover who he was before he made a commitment.

Following his parents' divorce, Rob also witnessed his mother's remarriage to another man who was not only an alcoholic but also cheated on his mother. Not once but twice he'd had to live through this nightmare. As a result, he made a vow that he would never cheat on his wife.

While this was music to my ears, I was also concerned about how Rob might react to my unfaithfulness of the past. By the time I met Rob, I considered myself a recovered cheater. I knew I didn't want any part of that life. I explained to Rob that the biggest reason for my cheating was my fear that my partner would do it to me.

In my prior relationships I never felt worthy or lovable. I expected men to treat me the way everyone else in my life had treated me. I was going to beat them to the punch. It didn't take long for me to learn that being unfaithful didn't help the pain but actually increased it.

Rob was nonjudgmental and sympathetic toward me. Being raised by a single mom and having an older sister gave him a lot of understanding and respect for women. He adored his mother. Although his mother's life hadn't been easy, she had given her children a lot of love and care. Like me, Rob admitted that he had spent a lot of time in childhood alone since his mother worked; but he always knew he was loved.

By now, Rob's mom had married again and had found happiness when she and her husband recently became Christians along with his sister Dawn and her family. He said that they had been so excited about their newfound faith that they had persuaded him to go to church with them.

Seeking God in my own life, I was pleased to hear Rob mention God. This really piqued my interest since I was on my quest to find God. I was delighted that we were beginning to dialogue about our budding faith. When it came to Christianity, we discovered that we were both seekers moving in the same direction. *Can two walk together without agreeing to meet? (Amos 3:3)*. "Did you like church?" I was curious.

"Yes, but I don't want to be a Jesus freak. I am committed to learn about Jesus, but I'm not yet ready to make a commitment."

"What's stopping you?" I was curious.

Sheepishly Rob admitted, "Maybe when I'm older, but now I just want to have fun." He feared that his life would no longer be enjoyable if he became a Christian.

I understood because until I met Chauncey and Scott, I used to think that people who went to church were all like the church lady portrayed on the NBC show, *Saturday Night Live*. I erroneously believed that if you went to church, you weren't cool.

Because I was still a seeker in my faith, I hardly knew what to say to him, so I admitted to Rob that I just didn't have all the answers yet but was very drawn to Jesus. I explained that I was a student of religion. Christianity was not a popular label in Tinsel Town. Most actors who were Christians were afraid to publicize their faith. I jokingly referred to them as closet Christians. I told Rob about my Christian friends Chauncey and Scott who were different from the rest. They didn't hide their faith and I admired the two of them for that.

We both agreed that it was one thing to believe in God, but to serve him was another matter entirely. Would the good times end once we became Christians? We feared so. Christianity seemed like a good thing for older people who had already had their fun and were ready to settle down or for geeks, but we were so cool. We were not ready to die to self. This process would take more time. Like readying the ground to plant seeds, the Lord was preparing our souls to accept him.

Both having suffered pain in our lives, we were bonded together in our quest. There was a deep connection and under-standing of the pain and loneliness we had both endured during our childhood years in our dysfunctional families. Rob and I were determined that all the things we had yearned for as children were going to be a part of our lives. I was honored that he wanted to introduce me to his family.

I was excited but nervous about meeting Rob's mother especially since he told me that she was very involved in her church and how strong her faith was. Would she judge me? I also was a bit hesitant for him to meet my mother. Would Rob judge me after meeting her? I remember a comment he had made about a previous girlfriend and how he should have known when he met her mother how she'd be. I didn't want to lose him. I'd start in a safer place, my father.

When my dad celebrated his sixtieth birthday in Florida on July 21, my relationship with Rob was going so well, I invited him to come along with me for the celebration. It was a no-brainer. I knew the two men would get along. After all, they were both police officers.

Just as I had suspected, they hit it off immediately. My dad had so much respect for Rob that my love for him grew. Seeing the affection we had for each other, my father pulled me aside to give me some great fatherly advice, "Tracy, when the time comes that you and Rob decide to live together, buy a new house together. It's not fair to Rob to move into a house you've shared with another man. Get a fresh new start."

My dad was helping me more than he may have realized. He was teaching me how to respect a man and not to make decisions based on whatever is most convenient but on what is right. The old Tracy would have whined, "But I like my house." Having my dad around is something I longed for my whole life—a father to guide me. I instantly obeyed his advice without question.

Shortly after we returned from Florida, I made plans to throw a surprise party for Rob on July 26. I invited all his friends to come and celebrate Rob's big thirtieth birthday. We had dated for about eight months, and I had told Rob I was going to treat him at a nice quiet birthday dinner with my sisters at Sage Brush Cantina in Calabasas. The Sage Brush Cantina is a fun place with good food and a live band that plays outside on the patio, just the kind of place that I knew Rob would enjoy.

After we finished our meal, I had planned to lure Rob out to the patio where all his friends would be waiting, but that night after our dinner when I suggested it, he said, "I'd rather stay inside where it's nice and quiet."

I began to panic. *What am I going to do? This is falling apart.* I knew all his friends were waiting outside, but I couldn't get him out there. I kept insisting and being as cute as I could be and said, "Please, it's hot in here. I really want to go outside." After several desperate attempts, I finally convinced Rob to go outside. I wrangled him out to the patio. As we meandered out there, all our friends were there with big banners and balloons and yelled, "Surprise" and then sang "Happy Birthday" to him.

Rob was surprised. He looked at me and grinned sheepishly. It was a beautiful summer evening, and we were outside listening to music and talking to our friends. I was so happy that I'd managed to surprise him after all.

When the time came for him to open his presents, I noticed that he had a funny look on his face, like maybe he wasn't having a very good time. I was concerned that Rob didn't seem to be enjoying the party that I'd gone to so much time and expense to give him. I just wanted to do something nice for him, but I'd blown it. "I should have asked him if he likes surprise parties," I leaned over and moaned to my sister. "He looks miserable." She said snickering, "Don't be ridiculous. Go sit beside him."

I sat beside him as he took the wrapping paper off the last present, which was from me. He had such a strange look on his face.

Did he not like my present? Or maybe he didn't feel well. He looked sort of pale.

I figured I'd blown his birthday celebration, but then he turned to me in front of everyone and said, "Tracy, thank you for a great party. This is a perfect day, and it would be even more perfect if you would say yes to this next question." To my surprise Rob got down on his knees and pulled a ring out of his pocket. He proposed to me right there in front of everyone. I was speechless.

Poor Rob, no wonder he didn't want to go outside. He had planned a romantic proposal at a small family dinner when suddenly all his friends appeared. This situation says so much about Rob's character. He didn't change his plans to propose to me; he just kept on course. Whatever the circumstances, whatever he's dealt with, Rob doesn't veer from his goals.

As Rob slipped the beautiful diamond on my finger, I suddenly realized that this was my third proposal, and the only time I meant it when I said, "Yes, with all my heart." Rob bought a beautiful, clear, perfect stone and had the jeweler set it on a plain white gold band telling me I could get any setting I wanted. I chose a classic Tiffany setting with two baguettes, one on each side. Thin, simple, but with incredible quality just like the man who gave it to me.

My sister Kristine knew about both surprises and she did a great job keeping both secrets. I had asked her to bring the video camera so we could have Rob's surprise on tape. Little did I know that I would be the one surprised. I must admit that I've watched it many times. Afterward we laughed because we'd both been sneaking around the other trying to plan our surprises.

When we got engaged, we'd been dating for about eight months. We decided to wait at least a year before we tied the knot. In the meantime we made plans to buy a house and move in together. We joked to our friends that we were going to get mortgaged before we got married. We were not yet commited to the Lord and at the time would pick the parts of Christianity that we liked and ignore the rest. Selectively, we would choose the commandments that we wanted to obey and ignore the ones that interfered with our lifestyle. It was the church of Rob and Tracy, not of God. Fortunately, we serve a merciful God, and he was tenderly leading us home.

I was getting closer to making a commitment to Jesus even though I didn't have the fortitude to stop having sex before marriage. While deep down, I knew it was wrong, I justified my behavior by sort of obeying it. I refused to have sex with Rob on Sundays. I justified my behavior, thinking, *It's not like I haven't before*, or, *I have been married after all*, or, *At least we are engaged*. It's just amazing how a crippled conscience can protect you, at least for a while.

Rob was what I refered to as "low miles." He had never lived with a woman before, nor had he ever had a long-term relationship. On the other hand, I had been married, cohabited with two other men, and slept with countless others. Not exactly your virgin bride.

Before we moved in together, I wondered if I should confess my sordid past to him, and I must admit that the thought was pretty terrifying to me. *Would he judge me?* In fairness to Rob, I didn't want to pretend to be someone else just to make Rob want me. This time I wasn't going to be acting the part of what I thought he wanted. This time I wanted to be genuine. I wanted someone to love all of me—the good, the bad, and the ugly.

Gently broaching the subject with Rob, I told him there were things I should tell him about my past. Self-confident in the situation, Rob told me that it wasn't necessary because he knew the person I had become. To my great relief, we both agreed that my past had already caused me too much pain and that we would leave the past buried. What a gentleman!

Prior to moving in together, I also shared my father's advice with Rob, and he wholeheartedly agreed with my father that we should purchase a new home together instead of moving into the one I shared with Randy. It didn't take Rob any time at all to convince me to go house hunting in the Inland Empire area. I had loved this quaint city at first sight.

We purchased a home together that had high ceilings and an open balcony off the upstairs bedrooms, and down below the kitchen opened to a family room. I loved it. Once we moved in, we had so much fun decorating the house together. The house looked great after we got settled, and we were eager to have our friends and families over for a visit.

Rob and I were in love, and I didn't miss L.A. nearly as much as I thought I would. Since moving, I was auditioning less and less. Although I had told my manager not to bother with roles I wasn't right for since the drive into L.A. sometimes took me a couple of hours each way, his calls to me had stopped altogether. I was concerned. My manager assured me that things were slow and there just wasn't anything I was right for at the moment.

I started to question what I wanted to be when I grew up since my priorities were shifting. Rob and I sat down to discuss my career. Since my acting career appeared to be over, perhaps this would be a good time for me to go back to school. I could work part-time and pursue a degree. I had been so disappointed when I left school years before, and now I would have a chance to complete my degree.

I was intrigued with Chauncey's faith just as Rob was with his mother and sister's commitment to the Lord, so we discussed attending church. God was tugging at both of our hearts.

Chapter 16

Coming Home

Softly and tenderly Jesus is calling. . . .
Come home, come home,
Ye who are weary, come home.
—WILL THOMPSON, "SOFTY AND TENDERLY"

We feared we would be judged at church. After all, we were living together and not married. Not to mention, if I confessed my sins, the walls of the church would probably cave in. I continued to search for answers in the Bible and seek God. Rob and I talked about the Lord, and we prayed, but we decided that we were going to put church on hold.

Unbeknownst to us, the Lord was surrounding us with people in our lives who could mentor and disciple us spiritually. Just as Billy Graham said, it usually takes forty people to lead someone to the Lord. Rob and I were racking up our forty people. Right across the street from our house we had met some wonderful neighbors, Joey and Marie Gonzales. Rob and I had hit it off immediately with them and their family. The more time we spent with them, the more we liked them.

Marie had offered a helping hand to me, and since I was new in the area, I couldn't have survived without her. Amongst countless other topics, she had talked about her church. Although she hadn't blinked an eye that Rob and I were living together and not married, I feared going to church.

It was evident that the Gonzaleses really loved the Lord with all their hearts, and Marie seemed determined to have us go with her to Inland Hills Church. Sensing my hesitation to accept her invitation, Marie explained to me that we are all sinners. *The one without sin among you should be the first to throw a stone at her (John 8:7).*

"You just come to my church, and I can assure you that you will love it. It is so different than what you are expecting."

I promised Marie I would think about it. A few days later there was a knock on the door. It was Rob's partner's wife, who I was becoming friends with. While we were talking, she mentioned her church. Was I ever surprised when she told me that she and her husband attended the same church that Marie attends! *Lord, are you trying to tell me something?*

Later that evening I brought up the subject to Rob. "This Inland Hills Church must really be a special place. Everyone seems to go there, our neighbors across the street, even your partner and his wife," I told him. "Your partner's wife asked us to go to church with them, so I thought I'd go. Would you like to come along?"

Rob didn't protest but told me that he had to work on Sunday. He also admitted that there was another area about joining a church that he struggled with a little. He wondered if God would understand some of the things he had to do as a police officer. "Cops have to be tough," he explained. "I can't just say to a perpetrator, 'Oh, that's OK. God forgives you for your crime.' A policeman is hired to enforce laws some people don't want to obey."

I told him I didn't know how to respond to that and reminded him that his partner and his family were members there, so there must be an answer.

I had to admit I was intrigued by everyone's enthusiasm for the church at Inland Hills, so I eagerly accepted the invitation of Rob's partner's wife to go there. As I walked inside the church on Sunday morning, the music had just begun to play and the congregation began to sing. As I stood there and recited the words on the big screen, the music opened up my soul, and I began to cry. The music was modern and the lyrics relevant. The singers and musicians truly were given a gift and instead of using it for fame and fortune, they were giving it back to God. I was humbled by this. The song we sang was about how much God loves us and forgives us. It was as though I was standing in the presence of the Lord. The sorrow inside of me poured out as I stood there and lifted my voice in praise to the Lord.

Hearing the words that Jesus loves me touched my heart so deeply. I certainly didn't deserve his love. I'd been such a sinner, but from the words of the song, I heard that he loved me no matter what I'd done.

When the sermon began, I took an instant liking to the pastor. Pastor Dave preached a message full of love, joy, and hope. What a gifted speaker this man was! As his sermon unfolded, my heart was softening to the Lord. This pastor was close to our age, and he had a great sense of humor. He spoke in a language we could relate to and shared a message we could truly apply to our lives.

There was something so special about this church and the people in it. For the first time in my life I felt as if I had come home at last. It was fun, full of laughter and void of judgment. Inland Hills is called a seeker church. It was the perfect church for us. Their focus and mission is to attract the unchurched and the unsaved.

Week after week the Holy Spirit began doing a wonderful work in my heart. I felt as though each message was custom-made for me. I knew that Jesus accepted me no matter what my past had been, as evidenced by this passage from John when a woman of Samaria came to draw water and Jesus asked her for a drink at the well. He told her about the living water.

"Sir," the woman said to Him, "give me this water so I won't get thirsty and come here to draw water."

"Go call your husband," He told her, "and come back here."

"I don't have a husband," she answered.

"You have correctly said, 'I don't have a husband,'" Jesus said. "For you've had five husbands and the man you now have is not your husband. What you have said is true."

"Sir," the woman relied, "I see that You are a prophet. Our fathers worshiped on this mountain, yet you [Jews] say that the place to worship is in Jerusalem."

Jesus told her, "Believe Me, woman, an hour is coming when you will worship the Father neither on this mountain nor in Jerusalem. You Samaritans worship what you do not know. We worship what we do know, because salvation is from the Jews. But an hour is coming, and is now here, when the true worshipers will worship the Father in spirit and truth. Yes, the Father wants such people to worship Him. God is spirit, and those who worship Him must worship in spirit and truth."

The woman said to Him, "I know that Messiah is coming" (who is called Christ). "When he comes, He will explain everything to us."

"I am [He]," Jesus told her, "the One speaking to you."
(John 4:15–26)

How precious of the Lord to choose a woman of ill repute so that I would know that He loves me in spite of my past or present. This passage, an example of how Jesus loves and accepts us, personally spoke to my heart. My friend Chauncey had been right—all the answers are right here in the Bible.

After attending this church, a familiar feeling swept over me. Just like the first time I saw Rob and that quiet still voice whispered to my heart, *There he is*, that same voice told me, *This is it, the church for you and Rob*. Like the Christian song, "I Love This Place," I knew instantly that this is where we belonged.

In the words of the earlier Scripture, Jesus told the woman to go tell her husband about the Messiah. I couldn't wait to rush home and tell Rob about the message and the church. I knew he would love it as I did.

I told Rob that upon walking into the church that first Sunday, I immediately felt connected. I love the feeling of fellowship in the body of Christ. Professing to be a sinner himself, the pastor appeared nonjudgmental as he explained how we all fall short. He stressed that Christianity is about a relationship between a person and a real God. "It isn't about religion or rituals."

In the past I was afraid that if I went to church the roof would cave in, but the pastor calmed my fears by the use of humor in his sermons. Mistakenly, I believed that I would stand before the congregation and recite my sins one by one, and they would throw me out when they heard my confession.

Instead the special people in this place held out their hands and welcomed me into the fold. God used the pastor's words so powerfully in my life to speak to me right where I was. Every message seemed like it was directed to me. In addition, the music amazingly healed my spirit.

Now Rob and I had a church to attend. I was wondering what God's plan was for my life. Did acting have a place in the life of a godly woman?

Chapter 17

I Wanna Be in Pictures

*A painter paints, a musician plays,
a writer writes—but a movie actor waits.*

—MARY ASTOR, *A Life on Film*

Most actors fear when they wrap a film or a TV series that it could be the last time they will ever work. The rejection is almost unbearable. "You're too short, too tall, too fat, too thin, too young, too old." The reasons you don't get the part are countless.

Since Rob and I had bought a house fifty miles from L.A., I needed to be selective with my auditions. It was over an hour's drive in the traffic to most L.A. locations, and I didn't want to make the trek three times a week to try out for jobs I wasn't really suited for or had no chance of getting.

For an actor there is nothing so wonderful as to work at your craft. The opportunities are limited, and it's a tough business. Just because you've had one success doesn't mean that you will work again. I don't know how actors who aren't Christian survive. Well, some don't. They turn to whatever it takes to numb the pain—alcohol, drugs, and even suicide. If they do have the fortitude to hang on, then they likely will have to spend most of their time working in another profession, usually as a waiter because that's one of the few jobs that will give you enough flexibility to take off for auditions.

I was one of the more fortunate ones who earned a living as an actor in commercials and an occasional guest star. I, like everyone else, was aspiring to get a regular part on a TV series or a film that might afford me a big break in the industry. I was working hard in my acting class and really beating the pavement to try to get a job, but nothing was happening. I had few auditions and didn't get any jobs at this time. At this point I was starting to point my feet in a different direction—God.

Unclear of weither I should go back to school or continue to pursue acting, I began to search the Bible for answers. One Sunday in the service, the pastor gave us a prayer to pray: "Dear Lord, I am your faithful servant, use me." I begin to pray that prayer often. I was beginning to feel that maybe this business had no place for the morally elevated. I was at a crossroads in my life, searching for a career in psychology or possibly law, and this prayer could not have been given to me at a better time. Every day I felt lost, I lifted the prayer up to the Lord. I knew that I wanted to do something to serve, but I wasn't sure what.

This prayer also helped me because it was about asking for his will in my life as well as praying for an opportunity to serve. I longed to discover exactly where God wanted me to be. Through this prayer I also found my passion. I wanted to use my acting skills to reach teenage girls to prevent them from falling victims to their sexuality and to help them find their self-worth. I began to pray for these teenage girls and asked God to lead me to them.

A few days later my manager called. "I've got a great audition for you, Tracy. Aaron Spelling has decided to produce a daytime show for NBC. This is huge."

"I'm there," I replied. Spelling had an amazing professional reputation, and I was eager to be a part of his new venture, so I prepared myself for this audition.

I read for the role of Tess Marin, who was a nanny for a wealthy family. I loved reading the script and discovering this evil character. Tess wasn't at all what she appeared; she seemingly was nice, but behind closed doors she was evil. In an effort to get money to support her young son, she devised an evil scheme.

The family who employed her as a nanny was a wealthy and powerful dynasty. In the story, the wife suffered amnesia and suddenly disappeared. Her family was naturally frantic to find her.

My character, Tess, found her; but instead of bringing her home to her family, the nanny devised a sinister plan that would benefit her, naturally, and not the woman. Unbeknownst to the family, their nanny, Tess, had a baby boy to support; but she had no money, so she had the woman believe the baby was hers so that she could become the nanny to her own son. Sounds a little like Moses in the bulrushes.

The woman's distraught husband was overjoyed to find his wife but shocked to see the baby in her arms. He wasn't even aware that his wife was pregnant. Of course, they loved the baby, who has all the advantages of a child in a wealthy family. Things might have gone along nicely, but eventually Tess, the nanny, gets connected with the husband's evil twin to plot to get rid of him so the twin could get all the family money.

Tess's personality traits were drastically different from any character that I had ever played. My favorite characters are ones that you can see their public self and their private self, and the contrast between the two. I prayed I would get the part of Tess.

God answered my prayer with a callback. A callback is when the casting director likes you enough for a role that they invite you back to read for the producers.

I prepared for my callback, and I thought it went well. I thought to myself, *I'm getting closer.*

I used to walk into auditions with the subtext, "Please like me. I can be whomever you want me to be so I can have your approval." I was learning that God approved of me and Rob approved of me so I didn't need the approval of strangers.

When I arrived, the room was full of the other actors who were trying out for the part. I decided to go outside the room where everyone was sitting. I stretched and relaxed. When my name was called, I went inside. I felt totally relaxed because I wasn't desperate for the job. I knew that my profession no longer defined my identity because my real identity was in Jesus. Even though I would've loved to work as an actress again, especially on this show, I trusted God for the outcome.

I got a call in a couple of days for a screen test. I'd made it to the third step. My manager warned, "You probably won't get it." He was usually so positive, but he knew I was going up against others who'd been on soaps before, and I think he thought I didn't have a chance. "Tracy, don't be disappointed, but I think it's unlikely they'll go with an unknown."

I refused to allow the words of my manager to discourage me; if the Lord's will was for me to get the part, then I knew I would. It was that simple. When I went in for the screen tests, they did my hair and makeup and then they told me to wait in the dressing room. I was the last person to be called into the audition. The person who was in dressing room prior to me had left the monitor on so I was able to watch the other actors' audition.

Praying for the first time before an audition, I said, "God, if this is your will, please allow me the circumstances for a good audition." I relinquished the job to the Lord. In the past I wouldn't pray. Instead, I would demand that God give me the job because I wanted what I wanted. Now I wanted him in control and his will not mine.

A couple of nights later, my agent called and asked, "How far is the drive to Burbank?"

I said, "About forty-five minutes. Why?"

She said, "You're going to be making it a lot."

To her surprise I didn't scream, laugh, or cry. But I've never been a demonstrative person. I don't celebrate that way. I just said, "Oh, great." She said, "Aren't you excited?" I said, "Yes, it is great." But for me it wasn't the end-all that it used to be. After getting the part on *Sunset Beach*, I was informed that our largest audience demographic was twelve- to eighteen-year olds. I was going to reach the girls I wanted to help in the ministry that I felt that God had called me to do. I also understood that my role on this TV program would give me the platform to influence others. I thanked God.

Rob and I discussed the logistics. I was excited and wondering, *What is it like to be on a soap? If I'm on a soap every day, will people start recognizing me in public?* I was happy because I had a calm assurance that this was God's plan for my life. God had given me a platform, and this time I would use it to glorify him. "Thank you, Lord. This is something I've always wanted."

❧❧❧

Working on a soap opera as a regular was a totally new experience for me. The best part was having a place to go every day. The next best part was having a place to park in L.A. OK, maybe the best is having a paycheck in L.A.

When I got the job, I was told, "Be prepared to go to work with your headlights on and come home with them on." Rob was totally supportive of my career, and he wanted me to succeed, so I felt no pressure about having less time to spend with him.

Surprisingly, their description of the long hours for my acting job was an overstatement. With exceptional producers at the helm, the schedule was perfect, and they never wasted our time. The actors on the show were assigned to either a morning or an after-noon story line. My lines were usually taped in the morning.

A typical day for me began about 4:30 a.m. I'd wake up, jump in the shower, and throw on my sweats. It didn't matter what I looked like because I had a cadre of professionals at the set to transform me.

In less than half an hour from the time I woke up, I was in the car heading toward NBC Studios in Burbank. I had to leave the house at 5:00 a.m. to be on the set by 7:00 a.m.; that's L.A. traf-fic for you. It was only a forty-five-mile trip.

Upon arriving at the studio, I reported directly to hair and makeup. Most of the time, I'd be oblivious to the artistic work being done on me in hair and makeup because I was reviewing my lines one more time. Going before the camera without knowing your lines is every actor's nightmare.

To date the most lines I have had is fifty pages in one day. Yikes! Yet I always learned my lines prior to the show. The brain is a muscle, and mine must have gotten real strong.

Following hair and makeup, we would try on our wardrobe that had been chosen for us by the costume designer to wear that particular day. A costumer would make sure everything fit, but if it didn't, she altered it immediately. The wardrobe department had also organized a Tupperware container of undergarments that we had been previously fitted for and left it in our room. They'd thought of everything because we had whatever lingerie we needed to make our outfits look good. Once I was dressed and the costumer had ensured my fit, I was ready to go onto the set.

After wardrobe we would go on the stage to get our blocking, the movements the director gives you. For instance, after this line cross over to the sofa and sit down. Afterward, we'd rehearse our lines and start taping. I always studied my lines, but I would sometimes worry that I wasn't as prepared as I should be. When it was my time to tape, I would open my mouth and take the actor's leap of faith. To my surprise the words just flowed from my lips.

After a morning of preparation and taping, I was usually done by lunch break at 1:00 p.m. I couldn't have had a better job anywhere. I loved my job.

Soaps are the closest thing to a normal job in showbiz. We shoot at the same studio all the time with no traveling. The show is scheduled for a normal workweek, five days per week with weekends and holidays off, which is a luxury when you work in television and film. I'd never been happier.

The producers give us our schedules ahead of time, and when you're not in the story line, they give you a lot of days off, but of course, you don't get paid for those days.

So my life on the soap was glorious! My mornings were spent doing what I loved; my bank account was full, and I had fans!

Sometimes when I was out in public someone would recognize me. One of the funniest experiences I had was at a restaurant. I went into the bathroom, and after I sat down, I realized that there was no toilet paper. So I did what anyone in that situation would do. I asked the lady in the stall next to me to pass me some. When I came out of the stall, she was washing her hands and looked up at me through the mirror and shrieked. "Oh my, you're on *Sunset Beach*. It's Tess Marin. I am going to tell everyone how I gave you toilet paper." Everyone has to have a legacy, I guess.

Before I knew it, this toilet paper lady was asking me to come over to her table with her family. As luck would have it, they just happened to have a camera, and I posed for pictures with every single person at that table. I can just imagine the caption in the scrapbook: "The day I met a soap star in the john and supplied her toilet paper."

At first when people recognized me, it would surprise me a little. I really would forget that what I do is on TV. I guess it still felt like doing make-believe in Nana's basement. When someone recognized me, I would do this whole mental check: OK, do I have anything in my teeth? Do my clothes match? Is my hair a mess? After all, you can take the girl out of the country, but you can't take the country out of the girl. I wouldn't go out and present myself like a star. "Who is your favorite designer?" they would often ask me in a magazine interview.

"Wrangler, of course."

A lot of times people would approach me when I had just left the barn, and I guess that I probably smelled just like a horse. This sudden recognition made me self-conscious, but I was also flattered by the sweet things they would say. All those wonderful fans made tough times in the business bearable. There were times I still felt like a disheveled little girl. I didn't feel I fit in the glitz and the glamour. I felt like I was trespassing in someone else's life and that someone might catch me and throw me out.

Once I became a soap star, my family and friends didn't treat me any differently, and for this I was very grateful. I had also been warned that friends, family members, and even strangers might write to me to ask for money, but that never happened to me. Some family members and friends watched and supported the show more than others. I have to admit the ones who made an effort to support the show were in my good graces.

One of my biggest fans was my sister Kristine. She taped the show every day so she could watch it at night. She's done that with every show I've ever been on. My Mom was also supportive, and she watched every day. My mother never missed the good stuff in my life or a crisis, but she just never could understand how important it was to us to have her around for the day-to-day routine. Fortunately, now she was beginning to get it and was trying hard to be there for me.

By this time Mom and Kristine were living together in the house I'd bought from Randy. When Rob and I bought the house together, I kept this one as an investment. Due to the financial pressures, Mom split with John and went to work at Frontier Airlines and had recently transferred to LAX to be near us.

I must admit that it was great to be an actress on a soap opera, but it truly did not affect my life as much as one might think. I remember an actor on the set who asked me, "Doesn't it feel great to be a star on a show. Don't you feel different?" I told him, "No, it's not like I just cured cancer, and I still have to clean my toilets tomorrow." I still feel that way today.

One of the neat opportunities I had was attending the Soap Opera Digest Awards at the Universal Amphitheater. This would be the first time I ever walked down the red carpet. Prior to the event the studio sent me to the designer who did a lot of the costumes for Spelling's shows to choose a ball gown to wear to the star-studded event. Trying on all the expensive gowns and accessories was like being a princess.

I chose a royal blue dress with a black bead design to wear, and the designer told me that *Entertainment Tonight*'s Nancy O'Dell had worn this same dress to an event. The dress was magnificent. I didn't know then how heavy beaded dresses are, or I might have chosen otherwise. I've never been a big jewelry person, and usually I'm under accessorized, but I chose a pair of clip-on earrings and a bracelet to wear with the gown.

On the evening of the gala, I went to the studio to get dressed and have my hair and makeup done by the staff. Several actors offered to include Rob and me with them in a limo to drive us to Universal Amphitheater.

Once we arrived, they'd call out our names, and then we'd walk down the red carpet and pose for the photographers. I felt so proud walking down the red carpet on my handsome husband's arm. Rob looked dashing in his tux. When he stood beside me, I felt like Whitney Houston in *The Bodyguard* with my LAPD SWAT cop behind me.

It was so exciting that I didn't want the evening to end. Several members of the cast were going out afterward, but we declined. Because of Rob's career, he feels uncomfortable in unknown social settings in fear of any illegal activities that might occur. He always worries that everyone might feel that they are being chaperoned. Also, I wasn't sure how long I could pull off the cool thing. As I said in the past, I never felt like I belonged in the glitz and glamour. Always leave a party while they still think you're cool.

It was exciting to see our photographs in several newspapers and other soap publications. I was beginning to feel like a real celebrity.

Another obligation for an actor on a soap star is to do interviews. The publicity department at the studio told me that a soap opera star must decide for herself what kind of public image she wants to display, but because I was new, I didn't have a clue.

When I first joined *Sunset Beach*, *Soap Opera Digest* said their fans wanted to hear from the newest soap opera star, and they arranged an interview with me. My first interview was exciting but also a little bit scary since I'd never done one before. Because I'm so open and honest, I worried that perhaps I'd said too much.

When I shared my concerns with the publicity department at NBC and told them I'd probably goofed, they assured me that if something came out wrong, it was fine because the soap community media is about building up their artists. They explained that the soap publications encourage the fans to like the actors on the shows. Sadly, that's all changed today, and the soap publications have begun to report scandalous news as well.

From then on, I felt confident about doing interviews. Ultimately, when that first article came out in *Soap Digest*, I was pleased with it.

Although I didn't really socialize with my fellow cast and crew members, they were all wonderful people. The crew members who knew us best were the hair and makeup artists. We always worked well together.

The only negative I found in being a soap opera star was its lack of job security. Being a new show, the cast and crew of *Sunset Beach* always lived in fear of cancellation. Plus the actor never knows when he can personally be written out of the script.

Success depends on the ratings, and in order to get high ratings, numerous factors are involved. Scheduling is one of the most important of these. If your show is up against a popular show, it's a long climb no matter how good your story line. The other components to a successful show include good production values, good writing, good directing, as well as a talented cast of actors. The great thing for me was that I didn't have to worry about these details because I had the Lord in my life. *This is why I tell you: Don't worry about your life, what you will eat or what you will drink; or about your body, what you will wear. Isn't life more than food and the body more than clothing? Look at the birds of the sky: they don't sow or reap or gather into barns, yet your heavenly Father feeds them. Aren't you worth more than they? Can any of you add a single cubit to his height by worrying? (Matt. 6:25–27).* For this reason I was able to relax and really enjoy the show.

Chapter 18

From This Day Forward

Two are better than one because they have a good reward
for their efforts. . . .
a cord of three strands is not easily broken.

—ECCLESIASTES 4:9, 12

I was greatful to my church for keeping me grounded with my success. God used the music as well as the pastor's words to speak to me right where I was. The more I learned about the Christian life, the more convicted I became. It was all beginning to make sense.

As we began to attend church regularly, Rob and I came to the realization that we wanted to honor God as well as to honor each other. How wonderful it was that no one had to tell us or judge us but that the Lord spoke to our hearts. We began discussing wedding plans right away.

Since Rob didn't care to have a big wedding and this was my second marriage, we agreed that we'd prefer a sweet and simple ceremony surrounded by the people we loved. I had learned from my first marriage that a marriage isn't about the wedding. At one point we discussed the two of us just running off to marry. "Why don't we just go to Vegas and get married?" I suggested one day.

"I want to have my mom at our wedding," Rob said.

His devotion to his mother was so touching to me. I'd heard a woman should observe how a man treats his mother because that is a clue of how he will love and respect his wife. Since Rob wanted his mother at our wedding, I suggested that we compromise and plan a small wedding ceremony.

Rob agreed.

I asked, "How about Valentine's Day? It's on a Saturday this next year. Wouldn't that be romantic?"

Rob thought so too, and we went to Vegas to check out the venues and the availability. After checking into several locations, we chose the Bellagio Hotel. When we told his mom of our plans, she reminded us that February 14 was her anniversary. Not wanting to infringe on her special day, we looked at other dates and saw that March 20 was the next available date, so we set the date. This gave us plenty of time to plan our nuptials.

I called my mom to tell her to save the date and she told me that she and John had reconciled and reminded me that this was their anniversary. What are the chances? How sad that I didn't know my mother and John's anniversary. They were married years ago in Reno, but we hadn't been invited to their wedding and I never remember them celebrating an anniversary.

It was too late to change the date now; we were keeping the date this time. Mom and John were excited and didn't mind sharing the date.

I told Rob that since this was a second marriage I didn't want anyone to give me away. This would solve a lot of problems and spare a lot of feelings. I also decided that I was now a woman in her own right. No one raised me, so no one was giving me away to Rob. I was freely giving myself to him.

In my search for a dress, I spotted one in a magazine that I loved. It was plain with a Grecian flair, and since my grandfather on my father's side was Greek and my dad is half Greek, I had Greek blood, so this dress was so me! The sleeves of the dress were long and flowing, and there was a band of flowers and leaves at the waistline.

I looked everywhere for this dress but could not find it. Contacting the overseas manufacturer, he wrote back that they would be unable to provide the dress by the date I needed it. I was bummed. Finally I had found the perfect dress, but it was nowhere to be found.

My mom wanted so badly to be there for me this time that she was determined to find the dress for me. She went to every bridal shop in Colorado in search of the dress. When she finally found it, she had to beg the owners to sell her their sample dress. What a blessing to have my mother involved in my wedding this time. The fact that she was the one who found the dress that I'd set my heart on was all the more special to me.

I wore a circle of flowers around my head that my sister Robin made for me. She had also made a lovely necklace with a cubic zirconium cross that hung from a delicate white fabric choker.

Once we arrived at the Bellagio Hotel, I smiled as the photographer snapped the photos. Kristine did photography for a hobby, so she hung out with us while the photographer took his shots, and as a result, we have a very special photo. The wind had kicked up, and the photographer who kept posing us in contrived positions looking for perfection didn't want to shoot in the wind. I just stood there and nestled myself into Rob's neck, and Rob just was looking around like he was watching over me as I stood there in complete peace for the first time in my life.

Kristine elbowed the photographer and said, "That's your shot." She was so right. We cherish that photo from our special day.

There were no bridesmaids. It was just the two of us, Rob and me. Rob looked breathtakingly handsome in his tuxedo. During the ceremony I couldn't contain the emotions I was feeling. I felt so grateful for the blessing that God had bestowed on me. I had taken the blessing of marriage so frivolously the first time. Now God had forgiven me and wiped the slate clean. The Lord had given me a second chance. He had blessed me with an amazing man who would inspire me to be the wife that God ordained. I listened intently to the minister read the wedding vows.

I hadn't known God the first time I married; this time I did. To be married and hear the vows and understand them for the first time touched my heart, and I began to weep. Five people came rushing up from the audience to the altar holding out a tissue to me, but Rob put his hand up as though to stop traffic and said, "Hold on."

Everyone just froze because my husband commanded such respect. He put his hand in his pocket and pulled out his own hand-kerchief to give me. It was as if he was saying, "This is my job. I'll be taking care of her from now own." Everyone laughed. I understood what he was saying; I knew that God had blessed me with a real man.

For our reception we rented the top floor of the Harley Davidson Cafe and had a buffet dinner. You should have seen us traipsing down the Vegas strip, me in my gown and Rob in his tuxedo. It was late Saturday afternoon, and the lines for a taxi were incredibly long. We just went with it. The Bellagio looked pretty close until we began to walk down the strip.

I grew weary, and that old familiar voice in my head crept up to taunt me. *You don't deserve this! You're going to mess this up just like you have messed up everything else in your life!*

I became sullen and wasn't my usual bubbly self. Was I doing the right thing, or was I heading down another road to disaster? All I knew was that every time in the past something that seemed to be too good to be true usually was. I felt like I was waiting for the other shoe to drop. Then I reminded myself of God's sovereignty, and the difference between then and now is that now I had God's guidance.

Since I was working on *Sunset Beach* when Rob and I got married, I had to get right back to work so we only had the weekend to honeymoon in Vegas. Although short, it was a wonderful time away, and all doubts I had were erased with Rob's love and tenderness toward me.

When you've been living together, most people think nothing changes when you marry. But let me tell you, when you take that vow before God, everything about that relationship changes. Having said our vows before the Lord, we knew the importance of staying connected to him. We knew that a marriage could not survive on our own strength. Sooner or later when life happens, and we knew it would, our relationship could easily fizzle if it was powered by human strength alone. When a man and a woman bond spiritually, God's love empowers their marriage.

To me the difference between living together and marriage is like the difference between blood and water. When I married, it was the difference between how I felt about my best friend and how I felt about my sister. No matter how much you love your best friend, your sister is your flesh and blood. After you are married, the husband and wife become family with God at the center of the relationship.

Once we returned from our honeymoon, Rob and I agreed it was time to make a commitment to the Lord. What a beautiful way to begin our marriage together to accept Jesus Christ as our Lord and Savior. Wwe signed up for the new members class and committed our lives to Jesus. We asked God for the forgiveness for all our sins. I no longer worried that Jesus would consider me unacceptable for his kingdom, for he had paid the ultimate price for my sins.

It helped to know several cops who also went to our church. Rob had no idea so many of his coworkers were Christians. It appeared that it was just as unpopular in the police workforce to talk about Jesus in the workplace as it was in Hollywood.

Under the pastor's guidance Rob also discovered that God supported him as a policeman when we read the following passage in Romans: *For government is God's servant to you for good. But if you do wrong, be afraid, because it does not carry the sword for no reason. For government is God's servant, an avenger that brings wrath on the one who does wrong (Rom. 13:4).* This was a big turning point for Rob in his faith.

Rob and I not only made a commitment for Jesus, but we were also committed to live a godly life. We enrolled in Bible studies, read God's Word, and prayed. Together we went through the classes required to become members rather than attendees. We were worshipping instead of wandering. We hungered for all the gifts that God has to give his children. We became even more spiritually bonded as a couple.

As the Bible teaches, Rob assumed his role as the head of our household. Several of the men in our church began to mentor him and he assumed the role perfectly. I thrived under my husband's guidance and headship.

After much confusion, I finally understood God's plan for marriage. Submission was not at all what I had expected, but it is an absolutely glorious concept when you are married to a godly man. I think the line from the movie, *My Big Fat Greek Wedding*, although humorous, is a great description of a submissive wife: "The men may be the head of the house, but the women are the neck. And they can turn the head any way they want."

Rob and I enrolled in an "I Still Do" Conference at Arrowhead Pond to learn how to keep our marriage covenant with God.

The Lord did a miracle in our lives. He restored all the losses we had endured as children; he gave Rob and me the gift of abundant life. It was ours for the taking.

Finally we were able to die to ourselves. No longer did we chase after our desires, but we sought the will of Jesus in our lives. In church one Sunday we listened to the pastor encourage us to discover God's plan for our lives. His plan is much more fulfilling than any plan we had for ourselves. The Lord knew exactly when I needed this knowledge because I would receive some unwelcome news on the set the next morning.

I will never forget the day. *Sunset Beach*, which we affectionately referred to as *Sun*, was cancelled. I was debating a director on how I wanted to enter a scene when Scott Sassa, president of NBC at the time, came into the studio to make an announcement. He said he appreciated all our hard work, but NBC and Spelling had decided not to pick up the show for another season. I turned to the director and said, "Alright, we can shoot the scene however you want." Ultimately, when *Sunset Beach* was cancelled ten months after I had been hired, all of us involved were sad.

My faith helped me cope. I knew without a doubt that God has something else yet in store for me. I felt sad for those who did not have the Lord, especially the men on the show who had families. This disappointment was traumatic, and a lot of tears flowed that day, especially for all those who had been there since the beginning of the show.

Thanks to mine and Rob's faith, I survived the cancellation of the show. I was so fortunate that we hadn't depended on my salary to make our house payments. Rob and I were frugal and had saved a lot of the money I'd earned. Fortunately, I hadn't allowed the show to define me either. My identity was in Jesus.

So what does an unemployed actor do when her show is cancelled? Go to auditions. My agent didn't get as many auditions for me as I hoped. Formerly employed on a Spelling production, I just assumed most doors would be open for me, but they were not. Where my career was concerned, nothing seemed to be falling into place. Since the commute to L.A. was grueling and I was becoming more involved in my church, I began to believe that perhaps God had another plan for my life than acting.

For awhile, I decided to explore other careers. Perhaps I would go back to school. My college career had been cut short for a lack of funds, and I'd always dreamed of going back to school. Since our show was cancelled just before Thanksgiving, I decided to stay at home and enjoy being a wife and homemaker over the holidays. Having worked continuously since Rob and I had married, it was a welcome change to be at home. We invited everyone to our home, and I entertained for the holidays. We had a beautiful Thanksgiving and Christmas.

When the new year rolled in, it was time for me to jump into the job market. It was pilot season, so my manager persuaded me to audition again. I was encouraged when I heard that Sara Buxton got picked up by *The Bold and the Beautiful*, Eddie Cibrian had booked a regular part on *Third Watch*, and Susan Ward had booked *Shallow Hal* with Gwyneth Paltrow.

Being in between jobs in L.A., sometimes I would feel like Noah after the floods, just floating along with no sign of land. I had to have such patience.

When my manager arranged only a few auditions for me and I didn't get any of the parts, Rob and I decided that perhaps it was time to try to have a baby. I figured it was time to have a baby—if no pilot, then pregnancy.

Chapter 19

Lullabies

Sons are indeed a heritage from the LORD, children, a reward.
Like arrows in the hand of a warrior
are the sons born in one's youth.
Happy is the man who has filled his quiver with them.

—PSALM 127:3–5

Only one month had passed when I missed my period. Shortly after I'd gone off the pill, Rob and I had taken a romantic drive up the California Coast for a few days. We hadn't planned on getting pregnant this soon, but God obviously had other plans.

While Rob was at work, I bought a pregnancy test at the drugstore to confirm my suspicions. Sure enough, it was positive! I wanted to surprise Rob, so I had to bite my tongue all day long because remember, *I conceal nothing*. When Rob came home that night, I was jumping up and down when I announced, "I have a surprise. You'll never guess!"

"You're pregnant," he said with a big grin. Somehow he just knew. He is so smart and intuitive. I told him I was indeed, and he was just as happy as I was. I'd soon trade the country tunes I sang for lullabies.

I called the doctor to make an appointment to confirm the test results. My girlfriend Heather brought her camera along and accompanied me to the doctor's office. When the doctor confirmed that I was pregnant, Heather snapped a shot of me, smiling ear to ear with two thumbs up. Until that moment I hadn't felt sick at all, but as soon as the doctor confirmed the news of my pregnancy, I felt nauseated. Unlike my previous pregnancy, this time the nausea wasn't a burden. I delighted in it. It let me know every day that I was pregnant and that God was giving me another chance.

Rob and I were so excited, but for the next three months I suffered with horrendous morning sickness. Thank the Lord for being unemployed! I never threw up, but I just felt seasick all the time. I would lie on the sofa all day long and force myself to eat. The only things I could stand to eat were hot dogs, Mexican food—Taco Bell of course—and pizza. After work Rob would come home and find me, still in my pajamas, sprawled out on the sofa with our dog Buster with an empty pizza box between the two of us.

I ate and ate, taking full advantage of not watching my weight. With my stomach growing, everything else didn't appear so big. It's no surprise I gained a ton of weight—sixty pounds! On my last visit to the obstetrician's office, I weighed a whopping 180 pounds.

As my tummy grew, Rob teased me affectionately, "Honey, look at your stomach. It's almost as big as your fanny."

I never took offense and would burst out laughing. Regardless of my weight, I knew my man loved me, so I enjoyed every minute of gaining weight too. He was unlike any other man in my life. To him my physical body didn't define my beauty. What a gem my husband is, and what a blessing it was that I was able to stay home while pregnant. My heart goes out to women who have to work. I had a roof over my head, plenty of food to eat, and an amazing husband plus everything I needed. It was a glorious time in my life.

We decided to throw a coed baby shower at a lounge in the Premier Apartments, where our friend Scott lived. It was a gorgeous place. We decorated the room with all sorts of baby things, and my mother hung baby pictures of Rob and me around a gift table.

We had a ton of people show up for our baby shower. As guests arrived, we passed around a book and asked them to write a special message to Baby Melchior. My sister Kristine took a photograph of each guest, and we placed it in the book alongside that person's message. To include the guys, we gave them baby bottles filled with their favorite drinks. What a hilarious sight to see those big guys drinking out of those bottles.

We got so many adorable little things for our baby. We could hardly wait for him to arrive. Now we just had to figure out what we were going to name him. I suggested names and Rob suggested names, but we couldn't come up with one we both liked. A friend finally mentioned a relative of hers had named their baby Kyle. Rob and I looked at each other and said, "Kyle." Finally our baby had a name!

Following the party, we had a blast setting up our baby's room. My hormones were raging, and before we finished, I became emotional. Rob asked me what was wrong. I told him I couldn't decide where to put the onesies and the diapers. "I can't even set up our baby's room," I whined. It was such a little thing, but it seemed like such a tragedy to me at the time. Rob cajoled and comforted me. Instead of getting irritated with me for my whacky emotional state during my pregnancy, he seemed to be amused by me. God gave me the most wonderful husband.

We chose a Noah's ark theme for our nursery and found a darling ark lamp. Rob put up a chair rail, and we painted the wall below in a dark blue jean texture and above, a light tan. We used bold colors throughout the nursery with a Baby Guess crib set. We purchased a glider for me to rock our bundle of joy every night. We were ready and waiting.

I wanted to take this baby out of the Crock-Pot and throw him in the microwave.

The doctor was concerned about the baby's size in relation to me and told me she wanted to induce me on my due date, which was January 25. We were hoping our son would be born on January 26 since Rob was born on June 26. Rob and his son would share half birthdays. When we showed up at the hospital to be induced, they told us there was no room.

"No room in the inn?" We couldn't believe our ears. The nurse explained they didn't have a room for me and advised us, "Go eat some spicy food and take a walk and then come back. We'll probably have a room by then."

It was so cold. Yes, California really does get cold. Rob didn't want me to get chilled, so he took me to the mall where we ate and then walked around. Afterward we returned to the hospital, and we got to stay this time.

The nurses wheeled me to my room and then rubbed something on my cervix, and my body responded perfectly. Suddenly, I suffered a terrible stomachache. Next I started feeling the contractions, so they put the monitor on me. Contractions, for those of you who haven't experienced them, feel like someone has put a rope around your stomach and is pulling on it with a MAC truck.

"How about an epidural now?" I asked as though I was ordering a Coke.

"Sorry, honey, it's too soon," the nurse replied sympathetically. Then she stepped away again to chat with Rob. They were just talking away while I was lying there in horrendous pain.

"Hello, I'm in labor over here," I hollered. "Did you forget about me? Isn't it time you checked me again?"

"Honey, I just checked you a few minutes ago. You've got to be patient. You just aren't ready." Then she went back to her conversation.

"Check me," I demanded in a much louder voice this time.

Finally, I convinced her to check me, and sure enough I was far enough along to get the epidural. A woman just knows instinctively. The nurse called for the anesthesiologist, but could I survive until he arrived?

Rob was trying to help by rubbing my head, telling me to breathe. It was irritating me, and so I grabbed him with all my strength and said in a possessed voice, "That doesn't help one bit. Do something."

Surprised, he look me in the eyes and said tenderly, "Tracy, think about the good stuff. You're going to meet our son soon."

"If you don't do something, the only person I'm going to meet is Jesus," I cried.

Rob assured me, "You're going to be OK, Tracy."

Just when I could stand the labor no longer, the anesthesiologist walked in and began inserting the epidural. In a few minutes I felt great. All the pain miraculously disappeared. For the next two hours I pushed and pushed. The medical team kept moving me in different positions. All of a sudden additional hospital staff members appeared in my room. "What's going on?" I asked.

My OB, Dr. Malik, explained that these doctors and nurses were members of the Neonatal Intensive Care Unit.

"Why?" I felt panicked.

My doctor, whom I trusted completely, announced that my baby was in trouble, and she was going to perform a C-section.

I'd taken a class called "Maternal Fitness" to train for labor, and I'd also done a workout routine to prepare my body for the labor and the birth. "A C-section? No way." I felt like I failed. "I can keep pushing," I assured Dr. Malik.

"It's not you I'm worried about, Tracy." The doctor replied seriously. "Every time you push, the baby's heart rate plummets. He's under severe stress."

"Do what you have to do," I told her. I didn't want to be cut, but when she showed me there was blood in my catheter and explained that was why she didn't want me to go any further, I wanted Dr. Malik to do what was best for the baby. At that moment I knew I'd die for my baby.

"Your pelvis isn't expanding. We have no choice. This is why I didn't want you go any further."

I was disappointed, but faithfully I put my trust in God.

The doctor had to push the baby back up to take him out. Then she performed the C-section.

When Dr. Malik lifted the baby out of my stomach, it was intense. The doctor told Rob to peek over the sheets and see his son. At first the baby didn't cry, and it was really scary, but then the sweet little thing let out the most beautiful cry either of us had ever heard. Rob and I smiled at each other. We did it! Nothing can compare to the first moment you look upon your baby's face. The birth of a child is the culmination of the love you have for each other coupled with God's love.

I was shivering and shaking so they took the baby away to clean him up, and then they stitched me back together again. Afterward they rolled me into the recovery room where I slept for a long time.

When I awakened, I saw everyone I loved gathered around me. This meant even more to me considering that Kyle was born at

1:43 a.m., and they were all there for the big event. This was truly the happiest day of my life. A few days later Rob and I took our baby home.

My sister Robin and my mom had stayed at my house to get things ready for our little family. Our homecoming was so exciting. Mom had put up an "It's a Boy," sign on our door and blue balloons on our mailbox. It was such a blessing to share this moment with my family.

Sadly, my poor sister Robin had struggled for several years with getting pregnant. First she suffered a tubal pregnancy and as a result had lost the baby. At the time I found out I was pregnant, Robin and her husband were waiting to see if their second attempt at in vitro was successful. After she learned that the in vitro had failed, Robin was devastated, so I was afraid to tell her my news, since I thought Robin always resented me. I always felt guilty for what I had. I felt guilty for being the "baby," for having blonde hair and blue eyes, and for having more than my sisteres. Whatever the reason, I finally had to tell her I was pregnant.

To her credit, she was awesome about it. Robin was so happy for me that she buried her pain to allow me my joy during this special time. At the sight of Robin's tender face as she looked upon my son, I begged God to send her a baby soon.

Although her second in-vitro procedure had failed, God had a plan. Less than a year later she was pregnant by natural means. My sister Robin had a precious baby girl. This baby was truly a miracle. Robin only had one fallopian tube and the one she had was clogged and damaged from her tubal pregnancy. God is faithful.

Coming home with a baby was an adjustment. I had a difficult time breast-feeding my son, but I was determined to be successful for the sake of the baby since the doctor told me it would be much healthier for him. Neither of our mothers had breast-fed, so they were no help, but Rob's sister Dawn came to my rescue. She had breast-fed all three of her babies and helped me tremendously. Kyle was nursing at last. It is amazing how incredibly painful breast-feeding can be and how little I cared. The pain was so excruciating at first that my toes would curl every time I did it. It didn't stop me because I would do anything if it would help this amazing baby.

Rob had taken a maternity bonding leave at the police department, so I had the luxury of having my husband at home to take care of Kyle and me. My dear husband refused to let me change a diaper for ten days. Rob really took care of him while I healed slowly.

I was such a wimp and had no tolerance for pain. I don't even have my ears pierced because I'm so afraid of needles. Since I had to have the C-section, it took a long time for me to mend and to feel normal. My OB told me that it takes at least thirty days for your blood to build back up, and she reminded me it was a slow process because I'd gone through two labors. I came so close to having my baby naturally; I almost had him out, but then I had to have a C-section. Initially it had been a real disappointment, but all that mattered was that he was here and healthy. Rob and I loved him more than anything in the world.

Once I began to feel better, I couldn't believe how much I cared about someone and how little I cared about myself. No matter how tired or hungry I was, I only cared about him. There was nothing I wouldn't do to make my baby happy or to comfort him. I realized that I had such issues of abandonment that I overcompensated with him. I wouldn't let him cry himself to sleep. I never wanted this child to feel alone or neglected or not a priority in our lives. I worried about him, and I doted on him constantly. I rocked him to sleep and held him even while he slept. I was exhausted, but I didn't care.

My husband voiced his grave concerns about how over-protective I had become. We fought about my spoiling the baby, but I explained to Rob that my deprived childhood influenced my motherhood. I further stated that I thought it was mostly in positive ways.

I relished every minute I was at home with my baby and was so thankful that Rob provided for me to stay at home. This was truly a great blessing for us all. I was happy and content and believed that this was my new life.

Chapter 20

An Unexpected Gift

To love what you do and feel that it matters—
How could anything be more fun?
—KATHARINE GRAHAM, PUBLISHER, *The Washington Post*

K yle was only five weeks old when my manager, Michael Bruno, called me. I felt anxious because I was far from being ready to work as an actress again for a number of reasons.

"I've got an audition for you, Tracy," Michael announced excitedly.

"Oh no, Michael!" I shrieked. "I've still got thirty pounds to lose."

I spared my manager the other sordid details—like the dark roots in my hair, the zits on my face, and the puffy dark circles under my eyes from lack of sleep. The tasks of a first-time mother, and my hormones were making me crazy. It would take a miracle for me to show up at that audition looking presentable.

"Stop eating and start moving, Tracy," Michael suggested. "There's a part coming up on *General Hospital*, and you're just perfect for it."

Wow! I thought I'd never work again. I recently had turned thirty, and that's considered over-the-hill in Hollywood. It's also a milestone where many actors stop working. "I'm a mom now. I'm old, and I'm overweight. They won't want me."

"I'm telling you, you're perfect for this role. By the way, how are your roots?"

We laughed. Having worked with Michael for ten years, my secret was out, and I was sure that he could probably picture me in his mind, zits and all.

I immediately sprang into action and called my girlfriend Heather, a fitness model and instructor, and asked her to propose a workout regimen and diet. I put Kyle in his stroller and pushed him all around the hills while Rob was at work. As soon as Rob would come home, he would kick me out of the house to go to the gym for an hour. "Don't come back until you complete that workout." He assured me that he and Kyle needed some man-to-man time so I wouldn't feel guilty over leaving my baby.

Though not at my peak, I was in better condition than when I'd first received Michael's call; but on the day before the audition I was nervous. At this point it had been a year and a half since *Sunset Beach* was cancelled, and I hadn't worked since. I felt rusty and out of sorts. Besides, Kyle wasn't even two months old.

To help calm my nerves, my sweet husband drove me, along with Kyle, to the audition the next day so I wouldn't be far away from my precious bundle.

With my hair done and makeup on for the first time in months, I was thinking, *I look pretty good.* But when I walked in and saw my competition in their skimpy little spring skirts, my confidence plummeted. Why had I ever let my manager talk me into this audition? I had absolutely no business being there. It was far too soon.

Needless to say, I lost the gig, but I had to admit I'd lost fairly because the girl they hired for the part on *General Hospital* was perfect for the role. At this point in my career, I had surrendered to God's sovereignty and knew that sometimes it wasn't that God wanted to deny me a role that I wanted but that he was working in someone else's life as well. When I lost a part, I knew that the part was the other person's destiny and not mine.

Rob and I discussed that because God had closed this particular door, it didn't mean that he wouldn't open another one in his timing. *We know that all things work together for the good of those who love God: those who are called according to His purpose (Rom. 8:28).* My failure to get the part turned out to be a blessing, for it was far too soon for me to go back to work anyway, especially since the show had a much more demanding schedule than a new mom like me could tolerate.

Vowing not to put myself in this embarrassing situation again, I stuck to my workout regime. If I was going to be the best I could be and walk in excellence for the Lord. My husband became my ardent trainer. I was down on myself, but he encouraged me that I could get back in shape by making sure I went to the gym.

After fifteen minutes, I wanted to jump off the treadmill. But I couldn't disappoint my sweet husband, nor could I cheat myself, so with God's strength, I continued to do the exercises. *I am able do all things through Him who strengthens me (Phil. 4:13).* I promised Rob I'd do at least thirty minutes on the treadmill, and I didn't break my promise. I felt God's presence as I struggled to get into shape. As part of my fitness routine, I strolled Kyle up and down the hills in my neighborhood.

Slowly the weight began to fall off. Just in time, too, because in a few weeks my manager called again to say there was another part

I'd be perfect for on *The Bold and the Beautiful.* This audition went so much better. But when my manager called the casting director, she said that I was too heavy for the part. I begged my manager to call the producer and tell him I'd just had a baby, and he agreed. I felt I should do more, but what?

As in all situations I prayed for wisdom. *Now if any of you lacks wisdom, he should ask God, who gives to all generously and without criticizing, and it will be given to him (James 1:5).* Just as his Word says, God inspired me with a brilliant piece of wisdom. I suddenly recalled that my girlfriend Chris Chauncey worked on *The Young and the Restless.* Her show was located across the hall from its sister show, *The Bold and the Beautiful.* I phoned her immediately and asked her if she would do a huge favor for me.

Prior to being pregnant, *Soap Opera Update* had featured me as one of the Top Sexiest People on Soaps. I had posed with my dog, a mixed Labrador named Buster, and it was really a flattering photograph. At my beckoning, Chauncey agreed to take the magazine with the photo of me to show them so they could see me at my normal weight. Chauncey took the magazine over to the producers at *The Bold and the Beautiful,* and the next thing I knew I got a callback.

I am a fighter, and just as I persuaded my first agent, Irena Kamal, to take me on, I had managed to procure a callback. It takes this kind of chutzpah to survive in Hollywood. You have to do your part even when you are waiting for God to do his part. The difference between quitting and letting go is quitting when you had the power to do something about it. I was determined to do all I could to get what I wanted and not to be attached to the outcome.

I had a good read, but I certainly didn't feel encouraged when I saw the other girls who were also up for the part. They were all skinny and beautiful, and I was still a little frumpy. I suddenly stopped worrying because I no longer found my identity in my looks. If I was right for this part and if it was God's will for me to have it, the part would be mine. Otherwise, I knew that God would have something better for me.

Maybe God's plan for me wasn't even acting. If I didn't get the job, I could spend more time with my son. Whatever his plan was for me, I knew it would be the most fulfilling thing for me.

A couple of days later my manager gave me a call to tell me that I had gone to the next level. They were going to give me a screen test. When I showed up for the screen test, I looked around for the other women who were my competition so I would know who and what I was up against. Normally everyone comes at the same time, but no one was there. I was puzzled. "Where are the other girls?" I asked the makeup artist.

"You're it," he replied.

I was ecstatic that my odds were so good, but I tried not to get too excited.

Before the cameras began to roll, I prayed to God for strength and peace. I aced the audition. My manager was right all along; I was *perfect* for the role. I got the part! I was delighted to be working again. This was more perfect than the role on *General Hospital* that I'd lost. God knew, and he used the circumstances of the other audition in my life to prepare me for the role he had for me. God is so good in his sovereignty. He used the *General Hospital* incident to kick me into gear to prepare me for this ideal circumstance.

The Bold and the Beautiful was so much more suitable for my personal situation. Not only did the half-hour format allow for more time with my son, but also the producers of the show ran a family-oriented company. The father, Bill Bell, created *The Young and the Restless* and then *The Bold and the Beautiful*, which his son, Brad, now ran for him. My mom, agreed to work as Kyle's nanny on the set. One day she thanked Bill profusely for allowing me to have my baby on the set. He replied, "I'd never want to be responsible for keeping a mom from her kids."

With all my abandonment issues, this kind producer's words touched my heart. I was more determined than ever to do a great job for the Bell family. He had the crew set up a crib and changing table in my room, as well as a TV and a refrigerator for Kyle's baby food. They even assigned me the dressing room at the end of the hall that was near the door to the outdoor balcony so Mom could take Kyle outside for some fresh air on a regular basis.

Trusting our son to my mother was a big leap of faith for Rob and me, given our colorful past. But the way she had helped me care for him since the day he was born, I knew no one else would make me comfortable enough to return to work. This honor and privilege totally melted my mother's heart.

The decision to ask my mother to be Kyle's nanny proved to be a great arrangement for us all. In many ways, her care and love for Kyle made up for the time in her life she had lost with my sisters and me. What an amazing time of forgiveness for all of us.

Not only was I able to do what I loved and have my son near me, but I felt that God had given me a platform to share his message of hope and resurrection.

Chapter 21

Forgiveness

For if you forgive people their wrongdoing,
your heavenly Father will forgive you as well.
But if you don't forgive people,
your Father will not forgive your wrongdoing.
—MATTHEW 6:14–15

After the birth of my son, I yearned to be the best mother I could possibly be to my child, so I really wanted to walk in obedience with the Lord and get my heart right with him. Although I had given my life to Christ and accepted his forgiveness for my sins, there were still some areas of my life that troubled me.

In biblical times the standard punishment for a woman caught in adultery was to be stoned to death. The men usually drug the adulterous woman to the center of the town to make a spectacle of her so the other women would see the consequences of actions and be deterred from this sin. On this particular day Jesus was in town.

*Then the scribes and the Pharisees brought a woman
caught in adultery, making her stand in the center.
"Teacher," they said to Him, "this woman was caught in the
act of committing adultery. In the law Moses commanded
us to stone such women. So what do You say?" They asked
this to trap Him, in order that they might have evidence to
accuse Him.*

*Jesus stooped down and started writing on the ground
with His finger. When they persisted in questioning Him,
He stood up and said to them, "The one without sin among
you should be the first to throw a stone at her."*

*Then He stooped down again and continued writing on
the ground. When they heard this, they left one by one,
starting with the older men. Only He was left, with the
woman in the center. When Jesus stood up, He said to her,
"Woman, where are they? Has no one condemned you?"*

"No one, Lord," she answered.

*"Neither do I condemn you," said Jesus. "Go and from
now on, do not sin any more." (John 8:3–11)*

Jesus no longer condemned me either. He had given the simple
command of "go and sin no more." I had been so blessed by my life
turning around. When your life has given you nothing but sadness
and regret, you become enlightened when you learn about what
Jesus promised. When you obey, you are rewarded with more
blessings and more abundance then you even knew existed. You
would be a fool to go back to your old way of doing things. Yet
I was still hanging on to a few things in my life.

One evening I was sitting in my glider holding my baby close
to me after he'd nursed. I looked out the window and saw the sky
full of the moon and splattered with stars as far as I could see. As
I looked up into the heavens, my mind wandered to the baby I'd
aborted. The realization of what I'd done suddenly overwhelmed

me. Holding my precious baby in my arms showed me the bravity of my actions and my sin. Children are indeed a blessing from the Lord, and I had taken the gift God gave me and wadded it up and threw it back in his face. I knew my baby went to heaven, and I knew without a doubt that Jesus would forgive me, so the time had come for me to confess my sins once and for all.

God had given me a second chance with a gift from heaven. Holding my baby lovingly in my arms, I looked up to heaven with a heart of gratitude and asked for forgiveness. I knew if Jesus Christ walked into that nursery right at that moment, I could tell him once again that I was sorry for that abortion. But do you know what he would say to me? "What abortion?" That's the beauty of Christ's redemption; he's wiped the slate clean of our sins.

I gently kissed the top of Kyle's head and then visualized placing my first baby in the arms of Jesus Christ. There was no more guilt and no more unforgiveness but total peace in that room that starry night. I promised God that I would be the best mother I could possibly be to my son, Kyle. I would give him all the things I never had. Kyle would know he was loved not only by his mother and father but also by his Lord, Jesus Christ.

Eight months later at our church, Rob and I dedicated Kyle to our Lord and Savior, Jesus Christ. He was dedicated alongside another baby, Aiden, who would become his best friend. Aiden was born to our good friends a few months after Kyle was born. Today the two boys go to kid's church together every Sunday.

In Elton John's song "Sorry," the singer says that *sorry* is the hardest word. I agree! The Bible emphasizes the power of the spoken word, and yet I see families all around me broken up for the sole reason that one person can't say "sorry" or another can't forgive. Fuller Seminary professor, theologian, and author Lewis Smedes wrote, "Forgiving is a gift God has given us for healing ourselves before we are ready to help anyone else."[7] I had forgiven myself. I knew it was time to forgive my family.

While my mom was working as a customer service rep at Frontier Airlines she hurt her neck swinging bags, and in another incident she fell on a wet floor. Another time she was taking an employee bus when the bus driver slammed the door on her. All three things happened within a short period. She worked until the last accident, but then she began to draw disability. John and Mom loved close by and were back in my life. It was as if the Lord was saying to me, "Well done my good and faithful servant; now how about forgiving your parents?" *Honor your father and our mother so that you may have a long life in the land that the LORD your God is giving you (Exod. 20:12).*

The thought of this made me squirm in my seat. In my therapy sessions Dr. Doctor had encouraged me to distance myself from my mother. I felt totally justified in not dealing with this issue. Now the Lord was telling me to make this relationship right. Surprisingly, God used John to begin the forgiveness process in our lives.

John was so happy to be back with my mother again that he became emotional. He came to me and apologized profusely that he was unable to send me to college.

The fact that he could validate my pain and have remorse was great for me. It is what we all want, someone to take responsibility for how they wrong you. It is so unproductive when people just defend their bad behavior. We all can justify bad behavior. There are people sitting on death row today that felt justified murdering someone. The Bible says that we should forgive someone who repents. When someone asks for your forgiveness, it is such a wonderful gift. What John had given me was a wonderful gift, but I was a bit disappointed that John only had remorse for not sending me to college—nothing else.

I longed to hear an apology for taking my mother from me. I also had to forgive him for not being a father to us girls when he married our mother. In the book *The Power That Women Have*, the author writes, "If a woman is grieving and broken in her heart, and a man is responsible for that grief, the only thing that will truly comfort her is for him to take responsibility for inflicting the pain. The only thing that will free him is the truth. The only thing that will free her is his truth. The only thing that will heal both of them is forgiveness."[8]

John became a husband only, not a father. I had to accept that he was only capable of that one apology. Perhaps in due time as the Lord works in his life, there will be other apologies.

Next came my mother. Because of all the uncertainty in my childhood, I have always felt compelled to appreciate every day and not take anything for granted. I lost my mother before, and it was the most painful thing in my life for me to live without her. It is possible that I likely will lose her again someday when she goes to be with the Lord. So it doesn't make sense not to have a relationship with her now because I'm angry with her for not being there for me through the years.

As a child, I longed for a relationship with my mother. Why let the bitterness of the past take away that chance to have a relationship today? My mother hasn't made forgiving easy as she still possesses some of her same old patterns. She accuses me of not letting go of the past, but when she brings her old behavior of the past into the present, I have a difficult time handling it, especially when it relates to my son. Where Kyle is concerned, I have zero tolerance for some of her behavior. I have to admit my responses to her behavior are not always appropriate to the situation. I guess I am a little sensitized.

Forgiving my mother was also a challenge because of her denial of the past she had inflicted upon us children. I know there are three sides to everything—yours, mine, and the truth. I was praying for God's help in the situation. It was just too big for me. Dr. Lewis Smedes also noted, "Forgiving our enemy does not necessarily turn him into a close friend or a promising husband or a trustworthy partner. We do not diminish the wrongness of what he did to us. We do not blind ourselves to the reality that he is perfectly capable of doing it again. But we take him back into our private world as a person who shares our faulty humanity, bruised like us, faulty like us, still thoroughly blamable for what he did to us. Yet human like us."[9] That's exactly what I needed to do with my relationship with my mother. I admit that I have a difficult time trusting her, but I pray all the time that God will help us. I know how much it means to him for me to have a relationship with her.

Slowly I could see signs of some remorse in the conversations we shared. When I told my mother that everyone had forgotten my tenth birthday when Pop-Pop went to the hospital, she reacted with sadness. When I celebrated my twenty-fifth birthday, my mother really touched my heart when she threw me a ten-year-old party for my birthday.

The party was everything a ten-year-old girl dreamed of and delighted a twenty-five-year-old girl. Mom hung balloons and passed out hats and party favors. My guests and I played pin the tail on the donkey and all sorts of fun kids' games. Mom even hired a magician. This was my mother's precious way of trying to make up for some of the losses of my childhood.

When I walked in, I rolled my eyes a lot and felt sort of silly at the idea of this party. To this day I struggle with showing appreciation to my mother. I know I am wrong, and I am striving to learn to accept the good in her. By her throwing this party for me, her actions said what words couldn't.

In life, when something traumatic happens to you, I think we get stuck emotionally at that age. For me it was when Pop-Pop died and Nana threw us out of her house, and for the next fifteen years I remained ten years old. My mom's throwing me that party allowed me to grow older. This birthday celebration was the beginning of my walk toward forgiving my mother.

I used to refer to my mother as an emotional terrorist. She would just attack you with emotional ammunition if you imposed on her or questioned her at all. She would flip out. She spent so much of her youth being told she was no good that the slightest suggestion made her feel like you were "attacking her." So it made a relationship with my mother difficult.

Another thing I had to learn was to realize that I had unrealistic expectations. I had to stop putting my mom in situations where I knew she was incapable of succeeding. I would just end up mad and disappointed. You can't expect a cocker spaniel to be a pit bull. She is who she is. Even today I'm learning not to trust her with matters of finances and timeliness but to trust her in areas where she excels, like being a wonderful, nurturing grandmother to Kyle. Another thing my mother does so well is supporting me. She's my biggest fan, and even though I thought she wasn't capable of being there for me as a child, today I can ask her for anything and she will do it.

This reality has had a profound effect on me. I could forgive my mother and still set boundaries to protect myself, my husband, and my child.

Being on the other side of the parent-child relationship, I have learned so much. I understood for the first time that a lot of my memories from childhood are viewed through a child's eyes. The way a five-year-old sees a situation is different from a thirty-year-old mother. The emotion from the memory stays the same as you get older, but I had to realize that I was holding onto childish thoughts and memories. *When I was a child, I spoke like a child,*

I thought like a child, I reasoned like a child. When I became a man, I put aside childish things (1 Cor. 13:11).

For example, I used to feel that my mother spent all her time on the phone instead of with her children. Now there are times when Kyle tells me I am always on the phone. Of course, I am not always on the phone, but to a three-year-old a one-minute call can seem like an eternity.

The other way Kyle helped lead us to forgiveness is that his birth encouraged me to have a relationship with my mother. I needed her and was even willing to admit that I needed her for the first time. She was so readily available to help. With all her faults, my mom is truly nurturing; and up until her divorce from my father, she had raised three girls basically on her own since my dad worked and went to school. She must have done something right; none of us ever had a broken bone, and I was the only one who even got stitches. As stressed as I felt with one child, I couldn't imagine having three. How did she cope in her early twenties with three kids under the age of five and a husband who was gone all the time? I became more sympathetic to my mother.

Also through my acting I developed a deep sense of compassion, which helped me complete the forgiveness process. As an actor, you constantly have to put yourself in someone else's shoes. No matter what kind of person others may think the character you are playing is, the character thinks he is justified. For example, a person who is perceived as rude and unsociable by other people doesn't think of himself in those terms. He sees himself as a person who is so depressed because he recently lost a loved one.

At last I was able to see where my mother was coming from, and I learned a little more about the childhood she had personally endured. I don't believe for a second that this justifies bad behavior from anyone; it just teaches you to be sympathetic and to put yourself in the other person's shoes. We must be accountable for our actions, regardless of our circumstances. There are no excuses.

My forgiveness list went beyond family. I also had to forgive all the men who had taken advantage of me, especially the men who preyed on a little girl because they felt she owed it to them because she was "hot." I needed to forgive my father for not protecting me. I realized that I had to forgive my grandfather for dying. Just as important as forgiving others, I needed others to forgive me. I had hurt so many friends and family members, and I had hurt myself, and most importantly I had hurt God.

Now I could clearly see that God was using the birth of my Kyle to help me complete the process of forgiveness toward my mother and the others in my life.

Chapter 22

Amazing Grace

Amazing grace! how sweet the sound,
That saved a wretch like me!
I once was lost, but now am found,
Was blind, but now I see.

—JOHN NEWTON, "AMAZING GRACE!"

By the grace of God, I am living an abundant life of full measure today. *A thief comes only to steal and to kill and to destroy. I have come that they may have life and have it in abundance (John 10:10).* It is also a miracle that the little girl who couldn't cry has discovered her voice. As the pages of this book have unfolded, it seems so impossible that a broken life such as mine, the life of a person who had broken all Ten Commandments before she reached the age of twenty-five, could be redeemed and blessed as I have been.

The late, great Rosalind Russell once said, "Acting is standing up naked and turning around very slowly." How true. You put yourself before an audience and risk tremendous humiliation every time you perform. Writing a book about your life, especially if you have lived a life of sin as I have, is like standing before a crowd removing each piece of clothing one by one and then peeling back each layer of your skin and removing your body parts until all that is left is an ugly empty carcass for the buzzards to nibble. I'm not exaggerating.

When God called me to write this book, I wanted to run and hide, but my obedience has required me to remove my mask and strip naked in front of you so that our heavenly Father can be glorified. That a life where the person broke every commandment before she was twenty-five can be redeemed, is truly a miracle in itself. It is a testimony to all of you, wherever you are in your lives, that your life can be redeemed too—that you, too, can experience the abundant life.

My transformed life is possible only through the death and res-urrection of Jesus Christ our Lord and Savior. And I invite each one of you who does not know the Lord, or perhaps some believers who are not walking with him in faith and trust, to come into a life of abundance overflowing with joy, peace, and contentment.

Today I have lost my latest job, *One Life to Live*, which I jokingly refer to as *One Life to Give!* Prior to this, I left *The Bold and the Beautiful*, and now I'm back auditioning again, beating the pave-ment with thousands of other actors in L.A. If God blesses me with a job, I will thank him for that great blessing. In the meantime he has given me an incredible ministry.

I'm influencing those young girls I wanted to reach. I volunteer on the drama team at the church, and I write, direct, and perform in skits on a regular basis. I also serve on the programming team. We design the elements of the service to frame the pastor's mes-sage. On several occasions I have gone back to the drama depart-ment at Ponderosa High School and have spoken to the students there. It has truly blessed me that the Lord has allowed me to use my talents for his glories. If I can prevent another young woman from falling into Satan's trap, as I did, I will consider my life worthwhile.

I also love being a mom to my four-year-old son, Kyle, and a wife to my loving, wonderful husband, Rob. Through the pain of childhood, I have taken the lessons I learned from being neglected and abused and have applied those to my parenting. The rewards have been great for both my son and me. I am able to give him what I never had. God's calling on my life as a wife and mother is the highest calling.

Although I'm in my thirties, I am still considered over-the-hill to many in Hollywood, but I am a *Perfect 10* in the eyes of my husband, my son, and my Lord. My heavenly Father sees me as perfect through his eyes. No matter what my career future holds, God is in control.

Perhaps many of you also suffer from sin or guilt. The Lord is waiting for you with his outstretched hand. There is no sin too great, no past so dark, and no secret so shameful that the Lord cannot forgive and cleanse with his blood. He can redeem your broken life.

The Lord is calling each one of you who has suffered along with me through the pages of this book to a more abundant life. Below are some great ways to let go and let God take control of you life.

- Accept Jesus Christ as your Lord and Savior. *For God loved the world in this way: He gave His One and Only Son, so that everyone who believes in Him will not perish but have eternal life (John 3:16).*
- Confess your sins to him. *If we confess our sins, He is faithful and righteous to forgive us our sins and to cleanse us from all unrighteousness (1 John 1:9).*

- Ask forgiveness and forgive those who have sinned against you. *Then Peter came to Him and said, "Lord, how many times could my brother sin against me and I forgive him? As many as seven times?" "I tell you, not as many as seven," Jesus said to him, "but 70 times seven" (Matt. 18:21–22).*
- Seek his plan for your lives through prayer, the Word, worship, and Christian fellowship. *"For I know the plans I have for you"—[this is] the LORD's declaration—"plans for [your] welfare, not for disaster, to give you a future and a hope" (Jer. 29:11).*
- Trust. *Trust in the LORD with all your heart, and do not rely on your own understanding; think about Him in all your ways, and He will guide you on the right paths (Prov. 3:5–6).*
- Stand on his promises. *Your word is completely pure, and Your servant loves it (Ps. 119:140).*
- Walk in faith. *Now faith is the reality of what is hoped for, the proof of what is not seen (Heb. 11:1).*
- Obey. *But Peter and the apostles replied, "We must obey God rather than men" (Acts 5:29).*
- Love. *He said to him, "Love the Lord your God with all your heart, with all your soul, and with all your mind. This is the greatest and most important commandment. The second is like it: Love your neighbor as yourself" (Matt. 22:37–39).*
- Give. *It is more blessed to give than to receive (Acts 20:35).* In the Bible, faith is mentioned 246 times, love is mentioned 733 times, hope 185 times, and giving 2,285 times.

Through these steps I am experiencing true joy for the first time in my life. As Pastor Dave described it, "There should be nothing between you and Jesus." In the past I could never laugh because I hadn't cried. The flowers in my life were unable to grow until I went through the rain. I learned that a dead-end street is just a place to turn around. I was on a dead-end street living in the world instead of by the Word.

As a child I was given little. I felt like my wants and desires were frivolous, so I lived in a deprived world. This world made me feel nothing but fear. I had no idea what an abundance God promises. I was so arrogant that I thought I was actually in control. I was like a child on a twenty-five-cent ride. I was pushing the buttons and flooring the gas pedal and turning the steering wheel. Actually, I thought I was controlling the situation. I held onto things so tightly. Now that I have let God be in the driver's seat of my life, I am freed of that. It was such a burden. I learned not only to ask forgiveness for the trials of my childhood; I have learned to be grateful for them. *Whenever trouble comes your way let it be an opportunity for joy. . . . I want you to . . . trust me in your times of trouble, and I will rescue you, and you will give me glory (James 1:2; Ps. 50:14–15 NLT)*. This is why I am writing this book.

This summer as I was preparing to write this book, which by the way I never thought I could do, at one point I started seriously doubting if I should even be doing it. Pastor Dave said in church in such perfect timing as he always does, "It isn't our ability as much as our availability." To God, my answer is always yes. As I look back through my Morning Pages Journal there was so much pain, confusion, and anger upon those pages, but I could also see the evolution of my heart and soul. It was profound to read. I wept for that girl I used to be, and I praised God for the woman I became. As I sat in my beautiful house on the hill with the most amazing husband and son peacefully asleep, I knew it was all because of God's grace. God has been so good to me.

One of the greatest blessings of my life is the close relationship I share with my two sisters, Robin and Kristine. The three of us live in the Los Angeles area with our families adn share holidays and special occasions with each other. By God's grace, we are all believers so we share our faith and have the privilege of praying for each other.

Watching my son Kyle with my mother and stepfather John is an inspiring example of God's miracle of forgiveness and healing. They are wonderful grandparents and Kyle adores them. My mother and I are very close and spend a lot of time together. Mom and John live close to use and are an important part of our lives. God is truly restoring the years that the locust have eaten. He is a God of second chances. My mother and stepfather are able to enjoy the unconditional love of a child through God's redemption. It is heartwarming for me to see how much my son loves them.

My father and his wife Sharon, and my four half siblings, are also an important part of our lives. After many long years of doubt, I feel loved and adored by my father. My father also treats my husband like a son—the two have so much in common. We spend a lot of time with them, visiting them in Florida or when they come to California to see us. They are also devoted grandparents to Kyle and he adores them too.

My grandmother resides in an assisted living facility in California and I also visit her regularly. I am now in a position to give her back some of the love she gave to me as a child. Recently, when I was visiting my grandmother, I was surprised to see my faithful friend Bob Feffer by her side. Bob has remained a wonderful friend to my entire family. This loving, generous man has helped my family and me in so many ways that he has become part of our family.

In spite of my problems, I forged some deep friendships during those tumultuous years I lived in the L.A. area. These Christian friends never judged me, but helped and loved me unconditionally throughout all my trials. Two of my girlfriends, Chris Chauncey and Heather Taylor, remain my dearest and closest friends today. Scott Reichert, recently married and he and his wife attend

Inland Hills Church. It is such a blessing for me to worship at the same church as my brother in Christ.

My former husband Randy has also remarried and has a family. Sadly, there was no happy ending by Bobby Payne. Several years ago he sister told me that he committed suicide. This news made me sad, but it also made me grateful for I realized how close I came to taking that same wide road to destruction that Christ spoke of in Matthew 7:13–14. *Enter through the narrow gate. For the gate is wide and the road is broad that leads to destruction, and there are many who go through it. How narrow is the gate and difficult the road that leads to life, and few find it.* I thank God every day that I found the narrow gate.

Reading my journal recently, I noticed that the last entry was five years ago. At the time I was still working through the exorcism, so to speak, taking place in my soul. I wrote how at the time I was angry with Rob for a reason so ridiculous to me now but seemed so earth shattering at the time. I was still growing. It was long overdue so I decided to make another entry:

> *8/9/04: It is the middle of the night. I couldn't sleep so I started to read the old pages. I can't believe it has been so long since I made an entry. I wanted to make one in case God forbid anything happened to me, and my last entry would be so negative.*
>
> *Rob and I have been married five years and have a beautiful son, Kyle. It's amazing to have just read everything that brought me here. God is good. Some of the lessons I still am learning over and over. As I reflect back, God has always provided. Onward and upward. Good-night.*

Notes

1. Christopher P. Johnson, *The Power That Women Have—Keys to Unlock a Man's Heart* (Indianapolis, Ind.: Fishnet Publications, 1998), 93.

2. Ibid., 162.

3. Darlene Marie Wilkinson, *Secrets of the Vine for Women* (Sister, Oreg.: Multnomah Publishers, 2003), 92.

4. James C. Dobson, *Love Must Be Tough: New Hope for Families in Crisis* (Waco: Word Publishing, 1996), 18.

5. Pia Mellody, *Facing Love Addiction—Giving Yourself the Power to Change the Way You Love* (New York: HarperCollins, 1992), 26.

6. Robin Norwood, *Women Who Love Too Much* (New York: St. Martin's Press, 1985).

7. Lewis Smedes, *Forgive and Forget* (Nashville, Tenn.: The Moorings, 1995), 8.

8. Christopher P. Johnson, *The Power That Women Have*, 162.

9. Lewis Smedes, *The Art of Forgiving: When You Need to Forgive but Don't Know How* (Nashville, Tenn.: The Moorings, 1996), 5.